# ARTHUR

# ARTHUR

## GOD AND HERO
## IN AVALON

CHRISTOPHER R. FEE

REAKTION BOOKS

*For the epic heroes gathered around my Round Table:*
*Emma, Chandler, Samuel and Maxima.*

Published by
REAKTION BOOKS LTD
Unit 32, Waterside
44–48 Wharf Road
London N1 7UX, UK
www.reaktionbooks.co.uk

First published 2019
Copyright © Christopher R. Fee 2019

Printed and bound in China by 1010 Printing International Ltd

A catalogue record for this book is available from the British Library

ISBN 978 1 78023 999 6

# Contents

Detail of a miniature of King Arthur taking a letter
from two Roman emissaries.

# Preface:
# Who was King Arthur?

Who was King Arthur, and why should we examine the myth-ology surrounding him?

The answers to these questions are complex, but we may begin to unravel this knot by following two main strands. First, the source materials for the tales of Arthur are rich in ancient mythic compon-ents; second, the medieval versions of these narratives developed over time into their own system of mythic, folkloric and legendary material. Simply put, the early court of Arthur is peopled with pagan Welsh gods and heroes of yore, which are transformed over the course of the Middle Ages into mortal heroes who fight monsters and embark on quests that we may organize according to categories we see widely in world mythology. In addition, much of the earliest Arthurian material takes the form of chronicles and saints' lives which – although not 'history' as we would define it – suggests that the figure of the mythic Arthur developed out of legendary accounts of the struggle between the beleaguered British and the Anglo-Saxon invaders who widely supplanted them after the final withdrawal of the Roman legions from Britain in the mid-fifth century.

Over the centuries, King Arthur himself has become a cultural icon of totemic power, and this book seeks to view the myths and legends of Arthur and Avalon from the perspective of comparative mythology. Looking at Arthur in this way may help us to understand why the hero of a half-forgotten battle some fifteen centuries ago still captivates our imaginations today. King Arthur has in fact gained the status of a quasi-religious figure: Arthur is both a cultural hero and a sacrificial dying god of sorts, and Arthurian figures, episodes, places and objects may thus be organized into and examined in archetypal mythic categories. A book of this length can't possibly examine every possible perspective on Arthur, but it can make a good stab at charting the most important aspects in an interesting and readable way, and can point the interested reader to resources for further study and exploration. That is precisely the intention of this book. This is a work addressed to the vast general audience interested in all things Arthur, and it is therefore designed to be accessible, engaging and illuminating for students and readers who would like a solid grounding in the myths and legends of King Arthur, as well as in aspects of comparative mythology as these can inform a study of Arthur and his world. The reader seeking a specialist treatment of Arthurian scholarship need only turn to the myriad such volumes available on countless related topics. The background research for this book was scholarly, and the endnotes reference a large quantity of recent and traditional scholarship on its topic, although as fluidly as is practical. It is my hope that readers will return to this tome repeatedly over time as they embark on new and varied quests in Avalon.

Whether or not one man gave rise to the towering mythical figure that came to be known as 'King Arthur' is a subject that will likely always evoke hot debate.[1] It is certain that the British did win some notable victories in their long struggle with the Anglo-Saxons, and such victories – gilded by the mists of time – have contributed to the aura of the 'golden age' associated with the Arthurian myths. In short, although there may have been a historical figure who has been remembered through the ages as King Arthur, we are unlikely ever to know that for certain.

Regardless of whether the man we know as Arthur once lived and breathed, the legend, folklore and mythology associated with this figure are very real indeed. A historical Arthur may or may not have rallied the Britons in their struggle against the Anglo-Saxons; what is certain is that writers from across Europe and throughout the Middle Ages cultivated and nurtured a vast literary tradition around the figure of King Arthur, and the roots of this tradition drink deeply from the wellsprings of very ancient legend, folklore and myth. And although King Arthur became a mainstay of French and – some-what ironically – English literature of the Middle Ages, the taproot of Arthuriana is firmly planted in Welsh soil, and the early Welsh narratives concerning Arthur are treasure troves of ancient Celtic mythology, as well as of medieval British legendary and folkloric details. For instance, the very name Arthur has itself been the object of considerable Welsh etymology, and one likely scenario suggests that the compound designator *Arth Gwr* reflects its bearer's identity as an ancient 'Bear Hero', an iconic cultural saviour that occurs in many traditions.[2] Notably – and again, some might suggest, ironically – possibly the best-known bear hero to contemporary readers is Beowulf, the epic hero of the Anglo-Saxons.

This book explores how ancient Celtic myths, in combination with early medieval Welsh legends and folklore, evolved over the course of several centuries – via many languages, literary traditions and countless pens – into a fully formed Arthurian mythology in its own right, complete with stories and subjects we might fruitfully compare to numerous god, hero, place and object myths that we could discover in any major mythological system. In addition, this book examines how the abiding appeal of this particular set of tales has been manifested in myriad modern works which take these myths and legends as their basis.

Before plunging into the deepest fount of Arthurian lore, a few caveats are in order. Medieval texts are very often hard to date, authorship is difficult to authenticate, and names, dates and facts can seldom be taken at face value. It is often impossible to know for certain upon what sources an author drew, and we must always question our own agenda and assumptions, not to mention those of medieval authors whose world we can only glimpse in always fragmentary and often misleading snatches. That said, we are likely to gain our surest grasp of what elements of fact may swirl at the bottom of the wellspring of Arthuriana by cross-referencing the major sources still available to us, noting where they agree and disagree, and drawing reasonable assumptions about why they may have done so. Wherever possible, the archaeological record – slim and suspect though it may be – might offer additional means to corroborate or refute various sources and assertions.

Detail from the 'Christian Heroes Tapestry', *c.* 1385, depicting King Arthur as one of the Nine Worthies.

## A Welsh folk hero emerges

A tantalizing hint regarding a folk hero of the Welsh comes from the pen of a sixth-century British monk named Gildas, who founded a monastery in Brittany, and who composed *De excidio et conquestu Britanniae*, or 'Regarding the Demise and Conquest of Britain'. As his title suggests, Gildas was concerned with the decline of Roman civilization and British Christianity in the face of the Saxon onslaught, and he is particularly harsh in his criticism of the weak leaders of the Britons in the decades following their one legendary success against the invaders. This work was written about a century after the final departure of the Romans and, according to Gildas, some 44 years after the Battle of Mount Badon, the great victory over the Saxons which is thought to have occurred around the year AD 500.[3] Gildas mentions one Ambrosius Aurelianus but no Arthur, although he does note a mysterious figure known as the 'Bear', which would be rendered something like *Arth* in Welsh or *Arzh* in Breton.

The earliest clear reference to the legendary King Arthur may occur in a Welsh poem called *Y Gododdin*, which is usually attributed to a bard named Aneirin, although the manuscript which contains the mention of Arthur is much later than its source. Arthur is not a figure in the story in any case, although he is mentioned in comparison to a hero of the poem. *Y Gododdin* laments the fall of noble warriors from the kingdom of Manaw Gododdin, the realm of the ancient tribe of the Votadini, which was located in the southeast of what is now Scotland. Acting to stave off the growing threat of Anglo-Saxon incursion, King Mynyddog Mwyfawr, 'Rich Lord of the Mountain', called to his capital at Din Eidyn British warriors from a number of allied realms. After feasting in this hall for a year, three hundred of the finest mail-clad mounted warriors set off to destroy their enemies; only a handful ever returned. Aneirin claims to have penned this account from memory, having escaped the slaughter by dint of his skill with verses. Composed soon after the battle in the northern stronghold of Din Eidyn – generally taken to be the Castle Rock of Edinburgh – this poem deals with an ill-fated campaign of the indigenous Britons against later generations of the Anglo-Saxon invaders, and thus has clear resonance with the literary tradition of the great battle at Mount Badon. Moreover, one of the two surviving versions of this text contains an oft-noted direct reference to the attributes of Arthur himself: a warrior named Gwawrddur is accounted in this poem to have been a mighty leader for 'feeding the black ravens', or slaughtering the enemy, although the poet is at pains to acknowledge that this Gwawrddur 'was no Arthur'.[4] The themes of heroism and steadfast loyalty are central to the poem, and thus this reference to Arthur has commonly been taken as a reference to ideals of martial prowess and leadership. In any case, this rather slight allusion to the great hero of the Britons in *Y Gododdin* may tell us more about the importance of Arthur as a symbol of courage and leadership than it does about a verifiable historical figure.

The symbolic significance of Arthur is more fully explored in the *Historia Brittonum*, or 'History of the Britons'. Written in the very early ninth century and compiled in the northern part of Wales at the monastery at Bangor, the *Historia Brittonum* claims to recount the early deeds of the population of Britain during the first few centuries after Christ. The author – traditionally thought to be Nennius – claims to have gathered and compared a large number of old texts in the process of compiling his history, and thus students of Arthur have hoped that this work at the very least reflects traditions older than itself, and does not simply represent a fabric of fancies woven together from the strands of the author's own imagination. Recent scholarship suggests that the *Historia Brittonum*, whether or not it recounts verifiable historical facts about an actual man we call Arthur, seems to reflect a discernible tradition about a legendary and mythic saviour figure of this name existing well before the compilation of this volume around the year 800. It is Nennius who provides us with the earliest surviving source for the story of the British tyrant Vortigern, his collapsing tower and the subterranean dragons which destabilized that tower.[5] The collapsing tower is an apt image of the decline of Britain under Vortigern, while the duelling dragons represent the struggle between the Welsh and the Saxons. Further, it is Nennius who credits the young Ambrosius Aurelianus with the discovery of those dragons under the tower's foundation; Geoffrey of Monmouth and other later writers attribute this prescience to the child Merlin.

## The great battles of Artur:
## the rise and fall of the golden age

The mythic golden age of Avalon classically is framed by a great military victory that heralds Arthur's rise and a tragic loss associated with his demise. Early references to the two great iconic battles of Arthur central to his mythology appear in the *Annales Cambriae*, or 'Welsh Chronicles', which survive in a number of copies, the oldest dating from around the year 970. These chronicles are structured along a dateline running from a year designated '1' to one labelled '533'. Corresponding to many of these years are entries which purport to record events from the beginning of the timeline to its end, a range which is generally acknowledged to span from AD 447 until the late tenth century. These chronicles take the form of short entries relating the major events for each given year and – concerns about historical veracity aside – in some cases these entries include material which clearly reflects traditions considerably older than the earliest surviving manuscript. Two episodes from these annals are of primary significance to the student of Arthurian mythology. First, in the entry for year 72 – generally taken to be circa AD 518 – the chronicler records that a battle was fought at Mount Badon, that Arthur carried upon his shoulders the Cross of Christ for three days and three nights, and that the Britons carried the day. Second, in the entry for the year 93 – which would represent AD 539 or so – we are informed that Arthur and Medraut fell at the Battle of Camlan.[6]

Arthur's great abilities as a warrior and his great devotion to God are detailed by William of Malmesbury in his *Gesta regum Anglorum* (Deeds of the Kings of the English) completed circa 1125. William also describes Arthur as a great leader, the heart and soul of the Britons responsible for reviving the shattered martial spirit of his countrymen, a role which culminated in the great British victory over the marauding Saxons at Mount Badon. Based in large part upon the work of Nennius, the *Gesta regum Anglorum* describes Arthur as a *dux bellorum*, 'warlord' or commander of the British under King Ambrosius, who had succeeded the ill-fated Vortigern. Noting the plethora of legends sprouting up around the figure of Arthur, William contends that he is a person worthy of the attentions of an accurate historian. It is therefore particularly interesting that William attributes Arthur's victory at Badon to an image of the Virgin Mary knit upon his armour, and that he recounts the hero's ability to vanquish nine hundred opponents at this conflict through single combat.[7]

Henry of Huntingdon gives a very early account of the concept of Arthur as a leader of mythic status in terms we might think of as the basis for the notion of the 'once and future king'. Henry's *Historia Anglorum* (History of the English) was completed around 1129, with notable additions made by about the middle of that century. Henry more or less follows Nennius in his summation of Arthur's twelve great victories as the *dux bellorum* of the armies of Britain. In Henry's 'Letter to Warin the Breton', which has been reliably dated to about a decade after he completed the initial version of his *Historia*, Henry mentions his discovery of a book which provides much more detail than his own history. Most importantly, Henry also mentions the so-called 'Breton hope', that is, the belief current in Brittany that Arthur did not die and will return.[8] The book to which Henry refers is none other than Geoffrey of Monmouth's *Historia regum Britanniae*, of which he includes a summation in his letter to Warin.

Geoffrey of Monmouth's contribution to Arthuriana is a fully formed and clearly articulated narrative of the life, times and death of Arthur.[9] Perhaps the best-known source of Arthurian material, Geoffrey completed his Latin *Historia regum Britanniae* (History of the Kings of Britain) by circa 1138.[10] A Welsh Augustinian – perhaps of Breton heritage – born in the late eleventh century at or near Monmouth, educated at Oxford and living until about 1155, Geoffrey was named Bishop of St Asaph in 1152 and displays in his work intimacy with the southeast of Wales, as well as some familiarity with Brittany. Geoffrey's stated aim of his *Historia* is a factual account of the lives and deeds of the kings of Britain beginning around the time of Christ. The high point of this history involves the deeds of King Arthur and his circle, and Geoffrey takes pains to recount the legendary and even the mythic elements of his Arthurian material as though they were historical facts.

From a mythological perspective, Geoffrey's account, while on the surface recapitulating legendary elements in a historical style, recasts the Arthur legend into its earliest form as a narrative with a

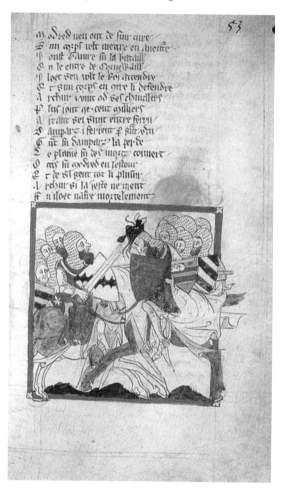

King Arthur is slain in combat; from a 14th-century manuscript.

series of clear heroic archetypes. From the miraculous conception of Arthur in the stronghold of Tintagel, in the midst of his father's enemies, to his great prowess in battle and from his mortal wounding in his final fight to his subsequent translation to, and presumed apotheosis upon, the mystical Isle of Avalon, the King Arthur described by Geoffrey of Monmouth is a hero of mythological proportions – far exceeding even the most fanciful accounts of a larger-than-life warlord who rallied the Britons against the Saxon onslaught.

Geoffrey's *Historia* is vital to the development of the Arthurian traditions in a number of ways. By beginning his account with a Welsh tradition borrowed from Nennius, that is, with the tale of the Trojan Brutus – a grandson of Aeneas and the beneficiary of a divine mandate from the goddess Diana to create a New Troy upon the shores of Britain, an island he bestows with his own name – Geoffrey places this peripheral insular realm firmly within the pale of the classical literary tradition, provides its rulers with a divinely mandated and impeccably ancient pedigree, and even provides an intriguing myth of origin for the very name of the island itself. Further, as the episode he describes between Arthur and the Roman Lucius illuminates, the classical foundation constructed by Geoffrey suggests a basis for the European political significance of what might be seen as a marginal and tiny island nation. Moreover, by placing Arthur squarely within the framework of a history of the rulers of Britain – and by giving him pride of place within a description of such a structure that allots Arthurian material fully a third of the text – Geoffrey makes Arthur's reign the vital lynchpin which holds together such an ancient provenance of classical civilization and the thirst for a courtly, literary genealogy for the Norman and French aristocracies.

While Geoffrey draws together such acknowledged authorities as Nennius, he also cites a number of subsequently lost Welsh sources. Most troubling is Geoffrey's heavy reliance upon a book he alleges to be of great antiquity and which he claims to have received from the hand of Walter Calenius, Archdeacon of Oxford. The existence of this mysterious ancient tome is not confirmed, unfortunately, by the citation of any of Geoffrey's peers. Such scruples about the existence and validity of source texts aside, Geoffrey's was an immensely popular work throughout the Middle Ages, as evidenced by the well over two hundred manuscripts containing the text which survive to this day. Still others are quite likely to have been lost, but in any case, in medieval terms two hundred is still a huge number.

Although Geoffrey wrote his *Historia* in Latin and in the style of a chronicle, the profound influence of the Arthurian material he collated and/or created upon later vernacular writers such as Layamon and Wace was to prove a vital step in the development of the genre of the Arthurian Romance. It should come as no surprise that the manifestation of Arthur that was largely developed in the *Historia regum Britanniae* was popular with the elite classes for whom chronicles, royal genealogy and, later in the Middle Ages, aristocratic romances provided a staple diet. Geoffrey's Arthur provides medieval British kings with a heritage of pomp, glory and the trappings of imperial conquest in a mythic package that privileges strong, legitimate centralized authority as both a powerful bulwark against external threats and a fragile institution to be protected against internal strife and treachery.

Although the *Historia regum Britanniae* set the tone for later manifestations of Arthurian myth and certainly was wildly popular by medieval standards, it was by no means universally praised, and certainly not all medieval historians accept wholesale the Arthur offered by Geoffrey.[11] Completed in 1198, William of Newburgh's *Historia rerum Anglicarum*, or 'History of the Affairs of the English', represents perhaps the best known and most significant contemporary attack upon the tradition of Arthur as it is manifested in the work of Geoffrey of Monmouth.[12] Although William's own text is concerned primarily with the history of England after the Norman Conquest, he spends a good deal of the preface of his own work lambasting that of Geoffrey. In sum, William criticizes the *Historia regum Britanniae* as artfully composed fiction masquerading as fact; in addition, the fanciful content of a work recorded in scholarly Latin, William claims, provides it with a covering of veracity with which to clothe its falsehood. Imaginative genius and artful composition aside, William condemns the *Historia regum Britanniae* as a fabric of lies and mocks those who cite and believe in Geoffrey of Monmouth as fools. More to the point, William saves the full force of his vitriol for Geoffrey's tales of Arthur, which he claims are complete fabrications, as is Arthur himself, who does not, William assures us, appear in the earliest sources.

## Arthur the flawed: hero and anti-hero in Welsh and Breton lives of saints

Arthur's growing mythic status as a hero was employed in some saints' lives in order to emphasize that the spiritual battles and heroes involved in religious literature were much more important than worldly struggles and victories. It is important to know that the saint's life was one of the most popular genres of literature throughout the

Middle Ages, and the *Vita Sancti Carantoci*, or 'Life of St Carannog', provides a good example of a saint's life which reduces Arthur's valour in order to increase that of a holy man. Composed about a sixth-century Welsh saint venerated in both Wales and Brittany – where he was known as Karentec – and dated to the 1100s, this text is relevant to any study of Arthurian mythology both because it contains an anecdote concerning Arthur and a dragon and because it is an example of the type of tale which presents Arthur as a manifestly flawed man and, not coincidentally, as an unsuccessful monster-slayer.[13] St Carannog, in contrast, seems all the more impressive, both as a truly holy man and as an eminently able hero.

Another example of a saint's life in which Arthur requires aid in subduing a dragon-like monster is *La Vie de Saint Efflam* (The Life of St Efflam), a Breton text concerned with the adventures of a sixth-century holy man from that region who, according to legend, was himself Arthur's stepbrother. In this case, Arthur had tried unsuccessfully several times to destroy a rampaging serpent, and thus turned to Efflam for help.[14] The saint promptly dispatched the monster for the king, and then miraculously caused the appearance of a spring in order to slake the terrible thirst Arthur had developed during his failed quest. According to tradition, this episode took place at Saint-Michel-en-Grève on the Côtes d'Armor, a detail that gives the story a very definite sense of place and thus a certain semblance of verisimilitude. Arthur's interaction with Carannog is similarly anchored firmly in specific locations in Wales.

One saint's life tells an ancient story of abduction with echoes as ancient as Persephone's kidnapping by the god of the underworld, although this tale is on its surface overtly Christian. The *Vita Gildae* (Life of Gildas), was composed at the monastery at Llancarfan by Caradoc in the 1130s. This work is important to a study of Arthurian mythology in that it claims to explain a source of personal animosity between the saint and King Arthur, which some have cited as ample reason for Gildas to exclude Arthur from his account of the Battle of Mount Badon. More importantly for our purposes, the *Vita Gildae* contains a fascinating episode concerning the abduction of Gwenhwyfar, a sequence which comprises an early example of a developing strand of the Arthurian tradition perhaps best known from the 'Knight of the Cart' narratives of Chrétien de Troyes and Malory.[15] In addition, Caradoc's introduction of one Melwas as the villain and his use of Glastonbury as the site of the stronghold to which Melwas retreats with the kidnapped queen are significant details, both concerning the evolving Arthurian tradition in general and regarding specific elements of that tradition which contain identifiable mythic material. Although in the medieval tradition this episode is told as a straightforward adventure, as we shall soon see, both Glastonbury and Melwas hearken back to far more ancient mythic sources.

### A company of brothers: introducing the Round Table

As iconic as the Round Table seems to a modern reader, it was an innovation of Robert Wace, an Anglo-Norman whose *Roman de Brut* was completed in 1155. Wace's work was the first significant attempt to translate Geoffrey of Monmouth's *Historia* into French; in the process, Wace updated a good deal of the material to reflect the tastes and interests of his courtly audience. Following the general outline of Geoffrey's *Historia* fairly closely, although working perhaps from a variant version of that text which has not survived for us, the *Roman de Brut* gives an account of the prehistory of Britain which is similar to that of Geoffrey. Wace does, however, add some material and delete other sections from his source; the most notable mythic material missing from this version includes the prophecies of Merlin, which Wace seems to have found difficult to explicate, although he does mention Merlin's foresight regarding the demise of Vortigern and the glorious destiny of Arthur.

Although heavily indebted to Geoffrey's *Historia* for many of its major plot points, Wace's *Roman de Brut* contains a number of significant alterations from its source material. Most vital among the innovations introduced by Wace may be the concept of the Round Table, the iconic gathering place of Arthur's knights at which each has equal standing.[16] Extending the earlier theme of Arthur's court as the maker of fashions, the destination for all who might aspire to join the ranks of the most elite warriors of the aristocracy of all Europe, Wace describes the Round Table as just such a gathering place for any knight who might wish to be thought courteous and worldly, or who might seek to gain in wealth as well as glory. In fact, any knight who appeared without the clothing, customs and courtesy current in Arthur's court, we are told, would seem uncivilized and boorish. Moreover, the Round Table described in the *Roman de Brut* was designed specifically by Arthur so that no man seated at it might claim a higher station than his neighbour, and all who were members of that select company were as brothers.

Another significant aspect of *Brut* to the student of Arthurian Mythology is Layamon's addition of mythical and magical elements. The newborn Arthur, according to Layamon, was the object of the attentions of the fairies, who blessed him with long life, martial prowess and the gifts needful to a great ruler. Completed in the decade before 1200 by a Herefordshire priest known to posterity as Layamon, *Brut* represents the first translation of Geoffrey of Monmouth's *Historia*

into English.[17] Heavily influenced by Wace's French *Roman de Brut,* Layamon's text is more self-consciously composed in the traditional style of the chronicle. Layamon's *Brut* is also profoundly English, both in its use of traditional alliterative verse forms and in its vocabulary and themes. Following Geoffrey of Monmouth closely on some episodes concerning Arthur's shaman guide, Layamon notes Merlin's role regarding Arthur's birth and also reports how the wizard transported the monolithic monuments from Ireland with which he created Stonehenge. Further, although Layamon excludes much of the prophetic material associated with Merlin in the *Historia*

Stonehenge is believed to have been assembled by the Beaker Culture
of the late Neolithic period, in around 3000 BC. Geoffrey of Monmouth
claimed that Merlin magically transported the stones from Ireland
to the Salisbury Plain to construct the stone circle.

Gustave Doré, illustration from Alfred, Lord Tennyson's *Idylls of the King*, 1867.

*regum Britanniae,* he does emphasize predictions of Merlin which foreshadow Arthur's everlasting glory, journey to Avalon and eventual return. Indeed, one of Layamon's primary contributions to the mythic lore concerning Arthur is his commentary upon the reliability of Merlin's prophesies. Although Layamon states that what one hears from the poets concerning Arthur is truth mingled with falsehood, concerning the greatness of that most outstanding of kings, the author of *Brut* is unstinting: according to him, the deeds of this king

– truly recounted in those annals just as they occurred in reality – were more courageous and wonderful than those of any other king.

These, then, are some of the most significant primary sources which feed the wellspring of Arthurian mythology. In the pages which follow we will attempt to chart the geography of Avalon upon a modern map, and as we do so we will be better positioned to locate some relationships between the literary and legendary Arthur and archaeological artefacts that help us to envision the physical landscape of Iron Age Britain. We then will explore how the court of Arthur is derived in large part from ancient mythic sources, and also chart how Arthur himself rises to become a figure of iconic status. Finally we will examine how Arthur, his knights and their adventures have been reconceived in contemporary literature and popular culture.

The Cadbury Castle Monument, atop Cadbury Hill, indicates the distances from this point to other sites associated with Arthur, including Tintagel, Glastonbury and Stonehenge.

# Introduction:
# Where was Avalon?

I f the legend we know as King Arthur ever did walk the earth, where in Britain might we pick up his trail? Ancient tales leave us clues that are more suggestive than they are definitive. The oldest tomes of Dark Age Britain are a patchwork of references to Arthur, his castles and forts, his cities and capitals. Through the science of archaeology we may search the landscape for confirmation of these battlegrounds and battlements. But even science offers more intriguing questions than it does empirical answers. Still, with medieval manuscripts as our guides across the rolling hills and vales of Britain, we may begin to plot some points in the geography of Avalon.[1] Furthermore, by delving deeply into the soil itself, we may capture glimpses, however fleeting, of the halls and walls that contained his fabled warriors.[2]

## Where might we find Camelot?

While Camelot is the name of the stronghold of King Arthur most familiar to modern readers, it is by no means the only such name; following Geoffrey of Monmouth, a number of early Arthurian texts speak of Arthur's main seat as being located at Caerleon, although other possibilities are mentioned, including Kelliwic, or Celliwig, which is cited in the Welsh triads. Camelot, or some identifiable variation of the name, appears in more than a dozen manuscripts, including some – although not all – of the surviving manuscripts of the Chrétien de Troyes romance *Lancelot*, the text in which it first appears.[3] The Vulgate Cycle, an early thirteenth-century series of

French prose romances, provides an interesting history of Camelot, claiming that Josephus, the son of Joseph of Arimathea, converted the citizens of that place to Christianity; Josephus is also credited with dedicating a shrine there to St Stephen, a church claimed in some sources to be the location of the marriage ceremony of Arthur and Guinevere.

Various Arthurian romances situate Camelot in a location near such notable geographic features as a great undulating plain, a mighty forest and an important river. This last possibility has proven particularly popular, as many scholars have taken the opportunity to situate Arthur's stronghold near a waterway dubbed the Cam, Camel or the like, thus providing the settlement with a ready-made source for its name. As tempting – and, to be fair, as plausible – as this hypothesis may be, there is little but circumstantial evidence to corroborate any such claim. The search for this legendary seat has been stunningly inconclusive, with possible sites as diverse as Caerleon, Glastonbury, Tintagel and Winchester, a wide variety of possibilities across a broad swath of Britain ranging from Wales to Scotland and from Wessex in England to the Cornish coast.[4]

Sir Thomas Malory identifies the location of Camelot as Winchester, some believe because of the Round Table constructed there in the thirteenth century; many contemporaries of Malory took this artefact to be the genuine article, which would explain why Winchester might seem a likely location of Camelot. Many students of Arthur reject this possibility, however, including such an early and notable figure as William Caxton, who printed Malory's work in 1485. Winchester, it must be noted, does in fact seem a somewhat unlikely historical site for the stronghold of a British warlord; as many have argued, this location was well within Saxon territory during the age which begot the original Arthurian legends. It is certain, however, that Alfred – the West Saxon king who eventually united all England against the invading Danes, and who thus exudes something of an Arthurian aura, albeit a somewhat ironic one – did locate his capital at Winchester, and thus Malory had good reason to perceive it as an ancient site of royal authority.

The search for the historical location of the legendary Camelot has long spurred extensive archaeological digs at a number of sites, perhaps most notably that at Cadbury, in Somerset, comprehensively excavated in the late 1960s.[5] Following the sixteenth-century antiquarians John Leland and John Selden, many interpreters of these material remains have pressed the case of Cadbury as Camelot.[6] The Iron Age ruins of that site are extensive, and there is little doubt that Cadbury was an important fortified British centre during the age which generated the Arthurian tradition. This hilltop site is impressive in dimensions and development: it encompasses nearly 8 hectares, with encircling outer defences that measure some 1,100 metres and the top of which offer a bird's-eye view of the country round about, which lies some 230 metres below the ramparts of the hillfort. The four-tiered earthen walls enclose a space easily large enough to accommodate a settlement, as well as, quite likely, the feasting hall and inner stronghold of a British chieftain of the late Iron Age. Indeed, hillforts such as this were symbols of status and power as well as fortifications of protection and refuge, and so it is quite likely that a significant figure was ensconced at Cadbury. Moreover, the crowning touches of a wooden and masonry palisade atop the innermost earthwork wall, as well as at least one rather well-fashioned gate, argue for the importance of this site and its lord, as do the remains of a great hall.

Given the intersection of Roman roads near this site and what we think likely about the British cavalry of the time, Cadbury might also have been an ideal centre for defence against Saxon forays and even attacks into the Saxon sphere of influence. Certainly there is evidence of a significant amount of power and prestige associated with this place; moreover, it is logical enough to assume that this site was favoured as a base of some major British leader(s) roughly contemporary with the events which gave birth to the legends of Arthur. The question remains as to whether there is any direct evidence linking this location to the figure of Arthur in general or to the legends of Camelot specifically. Some traditions dating from the sixteenth century or somewhat before may serve as slender support to such a notion. In the final analysis, however, there is no compelling independent evidence that Arthur's seat was at Cadbury, although the site certainly would have been an important and strategically located one.

Cadbury Castle, a hillfort located in South Cadbury, Somerset,
has long been thought to be a possible location of Camelot,
the legendary capital of Arthur's realm.

Another possibility for the location of Camelot is Kelliwic, or
Celliwig, a Cornish name meaning something like 'Woodland
Grove'.[7] The Welsh triads identify three great tribal seats of King
Arthur, including Pen Rhionydd, probably in Galloway in Scotland,
St Davids in Wales and Kelliwic in Cornwall. Kelliwic is a staple of
the Cornish Arthurian tradition and is regularly mentioned, appearing
in several of the triads as well as in the Welsh medieval masterpiece
*Culhwch and Olwen*, which places Arthur's seat there a number of
times. Regardless of its popularity in Arthurian sources, however, the
place to which the name refers is not entirely clear; the two main
possibilities include Callington, the popular choice of scholars and
hobbyists in the early modern period, and Killibury – traditionally
known as Kelly Rounds – the location favoured by most modern
scholars. Castle Killibury, as it is often called, is an Iron Age hillfort
in the vicinity of the town of Wadebridge; intriguingly this fortification also shows some evidence of use during the Arthurian Age.[8]

Overlooking the mouth of the River Camel, Killibury Castle
stands atop a mound rising about 90 metres above the level of the
water below. The site offers splendid views of the surrounding country
– especially down the river to the bay – and is an extremely defensible
position. Fortified as it is by a double ring of walls and ditches round

about – which still fill with water during the winter – and afforded excellent and unobstructed lines of sight in all directions, Killibury is a lookout post of a value far greater than its relatively low altitude might suggest. Furthermore, it seems to be at a conjunction of ancient roads, in close proximity to other lookout points and an old Roman post, and is situated advantageously in command of the river crossing point at the head of the estuary of the Camel. Archaeological excavation indicates that this site was used and reused for at least several centuries before the time of Christ; the evidence of occupation during the Arthurian age (a few centuries later) is more slim, but not non-existent.

A final possibility is that the term 'Camelot' could refer to a generic concept of a stronghold rather than to a specific location. If one accepts the traditional assertion that Arthur was a Romanized Briton or the scion of a house of Romanized Britons – and thus that his armies and power bases were likely to be associated with imperial military tactics and training – this seems a relatively plausible, if somewhat prosaic, possibility, especially given the Roman tradition of fort-building, in which each fortification was more-or-less uniform and structured according to a common model. Although this possibility is less than compelling, it could help to explain why so many sites are associated with Arthur's home base.

## Tintagel: birthplace of Arthur?

Woven as it is into the fabric of Arthuriana as the place where Arthur was conceived through the magical intercession of Merlin, Tintagel has long been another favourite as a potential site for Camelot.[9] Such speculation is not entirely without a possible basis: although the remaining castle ruins on this site date only from the twelfth century, this cliff-top eyrie was a centre of Dumnonian power from at least the 600s and may indeed have provided the power base for a local chieftain for a century or two before its emergence as a royal seat. Many of the elements of Arthurian myth surrounding this location, however, seem due at least as much to the inventiveness of medieval authors as to any solid claim to fame. Geoffrey's *Historia regum Britanniae* established Tintagel as a central site of the Arthurian saga, apparently due to the influence of Cornish traditions of approximately the correct vintage, and later medieval romance writers also attributed to this site the distinction of serving as the seat of King Mark, the royal cuckold of the Tristan and Isolt narrative. Tintagel Castle is described as enchanted in the twelfth-century *La Folie Tristan d'Oxford*, which claims that this magical stronghold vanishes once each summer and once each winter.

The site of a great cleft and cove between two stony headlands overhanging the Cornish coast, Tintagel, a name which implies something along the lines of the 'Castle of the Narrow Neck', is today the home of a small village and the ruins of a medieval castle constructed well after the Arthurian age. It is noteworthy that Tintagel is in the vicinity of Camelford; further, the cavern at the base of one headland has long been known as Merlin's Cave. Although the existing medieval ruins have no direct association with the Arthurian legends, recent archaeological excavation has revealed some objects believed to date from the time of Arthur. Although these remains originally were thought to indicate an early monastic settlement, scholars now tend to see this place as the home of an ancient stronghold – perhaps even a regional seat of power with administrative and governmental importance – in addition to its obvious defensive capabilities.

This iconic wall overlooking the cove on the east side of Tintagel is known as the Iron Gate. Dating from the 13th century, it protects the only landing on the island.

Tintagel Bridge, a graceful modern structure, crosses the sheer drop between the mainland and Tintagel Island: the only easy access to the ruins on the island, it amply demonstrates Tintagel's historical inaccessibility.

Until quite recently, modern scholarship had tended to call into question this place's traditional association with Arthur, because, although legend had long placed his conception at Tintagel in Cornwall, the castle ruins on the site clearly post-dated the period associated with Arthur by a wide margin, and assertions of earlier constructions on the same site could not be corroborated. Excavations carried out at Tintagel during the summers of 2016 and 2017, however, suggest that there was an active and opulent royal centre at this location during the late fifth and early sixth centuries; in other words, during the era when a Romanized Briton has long been thought to have fought the invading Saxons to a short-lived standstill, a British power base was, seemingly, in full operation. What's more, this sprawling palace compound, perhaps the capital of the King of Dumnonia, flourished precisely at the location where the saviour of the Britons has for centuries been claimed to have been miraculously conceived. Even more tantalizing are the range of luxury goods in evidence at this site, many of them from far afield and indeed from

*Overleaf*: The ruins of the Great Hall of Tintagel are situated almost directly above Merlin's Cave and overlook the Haven from a sheltered courtyard on a man-made terrace.

the environs of the still-powerful seat of the Eastern Roman Empire at Constantinople.[10]

Moreover, the emerging Romano-British ruins at Tintagel stand in stark contrast to the post-and-beam, timber, wattle and earth construction of their Anglo-Saxon neighbours of the same period. The latter might best be associated with archaeological digs of post holes and midden heaps that call to mind the great mead hall of *Beowulf*: images which evoke the so-called Dark Ages of an emerging Anglo-Saxon England. The palace compound at Tintagel, on the other hand, featured many buildings – at least two of them quite large – thick masonry walls, carefully constructed steps, impressively laid stone floors and other such evidence of architectural sophistication. Evidence of luxury objects of imported glass and pottery abounds at this site, as do remnants of expensive foreign delicacies such as wines and olive oil from the Eastern Mediterranean, the very heart of the new administrative centre of the Roman Empire.

There is, as of this writing, no evidence of the cataclysmic destruction of the Dumnonian palace at Tintagel, although recently uncovered clues may suggest that plague devastated it in the early seventh century. Epidemic outbreaks in the Roman world during the same period may suggest that the same cultural, economic and political connections to the Mediterranean which brought expensive goods to Cornwall might also have sown the seeds of the demise of this Romano-British centre – by bringing a deadly outbreak of disease from the same urban settlements in the Roman world which supplied the Britons with civilized refinements. In any case, although from a modern perspective it is tempting to see the final withdrawal of the legions in the mid-fifth century as the sudden and unambiguous finale to the period of Roman rule and influence in Britain, it is very likely that the Romanized Britons of the southwest areas of the island – desperate to protect their people and culture from the onslaught of the barbarous Germanic invaders and to cling to the vestiges of Roman civilization – actually continued to see themselves as a client state of the empire for many more generations. The legends of Arthur provide suggestive literary evidence of this, while the new material finds at Tintagel provide compelling tangible propositions that some elite Britons continued to value aspects of the Roman way of life.[11]

## Glastonbury: gateway to the otherworld

Glastonbury, we are told by Caradoc in Chapter Fourteen of his *Vita Gildae*, is derived from the Welsh *Ynis Gutrin*, meaning 'Glass Island'. Caradoc goes on to say that the Saxons translated this as *Glas Beri*, or 'City of Glass'. This etymology is fanciful, it is true, but it is perhaps especially noteworthy precisely because of the nature of that fancy. The notion of an island or fortress of glass was commonly associated with an Elysian otherworld in medieval Welsh mythology. Furthermore, this association was strengthened by Glastonbury's ancient identity as a holy site, as well as the fact that in ancient times this hill was virtually an island in the midst of a vast, trackless swamp. In this context, stories of Arthur's attempt to retrieve his stolen queen might be construed as a hero's quest to the otherworld, an Orpheus-like journey to the realm of the Lord of the Underworld to seek and recapture lost love. In fact, this theme was a popular one in the Middle Ages, and recurs in numerous texts related to the Arthurian tradition, perhaps most famously, if a bit obliquely, in Chaucer's *Wife of Bath's Tale*. Indeed, the genre of the medieval romance has, in *Sir Orfeo*, a blatant retelling of the Orpheus myth. This reflects a widespread tradition in Britain and France that illustrates a strong Celtic influence concerning the situation and population of this frightening alternate universe.

We find just such a tale in Chapter Ten of the *Vita Gildae*, in which we are told that the saint helped the Abbot of Glastonbury to bring about peace between Arthur and Melwas, the Lord of the Summer Country, who had stolen away and raped Gwenhwyfar, Arthur's queen. Melwas had secreted his prisoner away in his stronghold at Glastonbury, which was surrounded by impenetrable tracts of wetland, river bottom and marsh. Arthur searched for his lost wife for an entire year, and when he discovered where she was being held he prepared to attack his enemy with a mighty army. As the two antagonists prepared for battle, the abbot, his advisors and Gildas intervened, and managed to arrange the peaceful and honourable return of Gwenhwyfar to Arthur. For this service both kings bestowed considerable gifts of land upon the abbey; furthermore, the abbot imposed upon them a lasting peace and reconciliation, forcing from each an oath never to desecrate the sacred environs of Glastonbury.

This tale of Gwenhwyfar's abduction seems – on the surface – a straightforward story of strife between two lords, a conflict brought about by means of the unseemly and yet not at all uncommon detail of the snatching and ravishing of the queen. The entire episode seems to provide little but an occasion for the Abbott of Glastonbury – and, we are to suppose, by extension Gildas himself – to show merit in mediating arbitration, putting possible budding romance themes to one side. Scratch that surface, however, and a wealth of mythic material emerges. Melwas, or Melvas, who is known to readers of later Arthurian romance as Meleagant, is the 'noble youth' or 'ruler of death' who reigns in *aestiva regione*, that is, in the 'summer country', which we might better understand to be the land of the fairies or the ever temperate regions of the ancient Celtic otherworld. The stronghold of that realm according to the *Vita Gildae* is Glastonbury, the site, we learn from William of Malmesbury, of the *Insula Avallonia*, the 'Island of Apples', which will later become known as Avalon and will, after his final battle, provide Arthur with a supernatural resting place until his return to the world of men.

The fact that Gildas brokers Gwenhwyfar's return in this version of the 'stolen wife' motif has been thought to emphasize Arthur's

Glastonbury Tor has been a sacred site since ancient times. Glimpsed through the trees in the distance, it is clear how starkly Glastonbury Tor rises up to loom over the surrounding countryside.

St Michael's Tower, on top of Glastonbury Tor, marks the remains
of a medieval church built on the location of much earlier constructions.
The Arthurian stories of King Melwas of the 'Summer Country' associated
with this place may suggest an ancient pagan heritage.

insufficient abilities, but in fact it might be more fair to note that this
represents another saint's life – one more example of a widespread
tradition – which uses Arthur more or less as a foil to emphasize the
greatness of the holy hero at the expense of the secular soldier. In
addition, given the otherworldly tenor of Melwas and his realm, it
might be argued that, in an overtly Christian story such as a saint's
life, it is to be expected that a servant of God would be required to
counteract the powers of the otherworld, which we might expect to
have at the very least a whiff of the demonic about them.

William of Malmesbury gives us more information about Arthur's
resting place and its proximity to Glastonbury. In his *Gesta regum
Anglorum* (Deeds of the Kings of the English), completed circa 1125,
William simply notes that Arthur's return was prophesied; this lack
of specific information is largely due to the fact that Arthur's grave
was, as of that writing, yet undiscovered. However, in his *De antiquitate
Glastoniensis ecclesiae* (Concerning the Antiquity of the Church at
Glastonbury), finished around 1135, William offers a possible clue as

to Arthur's whereabouts when he provides a concrete location for the Isle of Avalon, which is often cited as the place Arthur was taken after his final battle. William reads *Insula Avallonia* as 'Apple Island'.[12] It was so named, he informs us, by one King Glasteing, who founded a stronghold where he found his sow browsing under an apple tree (*avalla* is a Welsh term for 'apple'). This, according to William, came to be the site of Glastonbury, most probably named, he would have us believe, for King Glasteing himself. In any case, this location seems most likely to have been a sacred place for time out of mind; archaeology suggests a very old Celtic settlement on the site, which later became home to arguably the earliest Christian centre in Britain.[13] As we have seen, Glastonbury was in ancient days rendered nearly an island by encircling swamps and marshes, which explains why Glasteing referred to this *Avallonia* as an *insula*. Finally, Glastonbury is a place of special note because of its long-standing legendary and mythic associations with Arthur; the same may be said of Avalon, which is – as William's work so aptly makes clear – sometimes conflated with Glastonbury.[14]

## The search for Mount Badon: the battle that created King Arthur

Born in the very late fifth century and living some 75 years, Gildas was a monk supposed to have been a native of what is now southwest Scotland. By his own account, Gildas composed his *De excidio et conquestu Britanniae* (Concerning the Ruin and Conquest of Britain) some 44 years after the date he gives for the Battle of Mount Badon, which he places in the year of his own birth.[15] For a variety of solid reasons, scholars commonly assign the date of this text to the mid-sixth century. In some ways Gildas provides the earliest historically concerned account of major events traditionally associated with the shadowy figure who would come to be known as Arthur, but in other ways this work seems almost self-consciously designed to be excluded from just such a tradition. No Arthur is mentioned by name, for example, and instead of the hero of Mount Badon, the leader held up as the hero for British adoration and emulation is, as we have seen, Ambrosius Aurelianus.

Some have asserted that, modern conventions of editing aside, Gildas may indeed suggest that the hero of Badon was this self-same Ambrosius. Be that as it may, Gildas laments the decline of the heroism and leadership of the British since the time of Ambrosius and remarks that – as the grandchildren of that greatest generation were far lesser men than their sires – it was to be expected that Mount Badon marked the last hurrah of the Roman civilization bequeathed to the British.[16] That these latter-day Britons were nothing to boast about is marked by the fact that Gildas steadfastly refuses to name any of them, even concerning the great watershed moment that he acknowledges Badon to be. Moreover, Gildas makes no attempt to compile history as such – although his work is prefaced by a thumbnail sketch of major events in Britain from the first century after Christ down to his own day – but is more interested in charting the excesses and frailties of the rulers of Britain, which Gildas cites as the impetus for the wrath of God brought down upon this sinful insular Israel in the form of the scourge of the Saxons. Such an apocalyptic interpretation of events represents a relatively early manifestation of a medieval commonplace which reasserts itself, for example, in the reproachful sermons of Anglo-Saxon clerics in the face of the Viking raids, and again during the time of the Black Death.

The British decline, according to Gildas, became precipitous after the withdrawal of the last of the Roman legions, a catastrophic event that led to the invitation of Saxon mercenaries into British lands to aid against other marauders, notably the Picts. Although Gildas does not name the foolhardy leader responsible for this rash act, later texts, including that of the Venerable Bede and the *Anglo-Saxon Chronicle*, cite Vortigern.[17] These mercenaries inevitably came into conflict with their employers over wages and supplies, and the end result was a new and more dangerous enemy right in the midst of the British. Having harried the countryside far and wide, the Saxons fell back into their camps, and were eventually soundly defeated – although not destroyed – in the Battle of Mount Badon, during which the British may have had the advantage of a leader in the mould of the mighty Ambrosius Aurelianus, although the text does not tell us for certain.

The tenor of the work as a whole echoes in this notable silence, which damns with faint praise. Even this unnamed leader, we are left to believe, pales in comparison with a warrior the likes of Ambrosius, who himself represents the last of the great Roman stock. Moreover, Gildas not only mourns the passing of this hero himself, as well as lamenting the mediocre talents of his successors, but decries the lack of wisdom of Gildas's contemporaries to live according to God's law and to learn from their mistakes. Gildas informs us that this battle ended – for a time – wars against outsiders; civil wars, including, ostensibly, the Battle of Camlan, at which Arthur is said to have perished, seem to have continued unabated, evidence which speaks eloquently to the explicit invective point which Gildas was attempting to hammer home. Although Arthur is notably unmentioned in this work, the messianic aspects of the Arthurian myth later would be founded upon the pattern of decadence and revival, and imperilment and deliverance underscored by Gildas.

Gildas himself later gained legendary status in the British literary tradition, appearing in *Culhwch and Olwen* and in the work of William of Malmesbury. More interestingly, Gildas is the subject of hagiography by Caradoc of Llancarfan: combining the trappings of an early romance with the genre of the saint's life, Caradoc's *Vita Gildae* is notable in the present context because it purports to recount the personal animosity between Arthur and Gildas. This alleged animus has on occasion been cited as reason enough for the absence of Arthur from the account of the Battle of Mount Badon recorded by Gildas. Though such a claim certainly falls short of incontrovertible evidence, it is undoubtedly true that both Caradoc and William link the legendary figure of Gildas with Glastonbury, and thus place him within the pale of Arthurian legend proper.

Perhaps most importantly, Gildas was perceived by later writers to be a historical source of great note. The Venerable Bede, to cite perhaps the most crucial example of this trend, used the work of Gildas in the compilation of his own attempt to record the early history of the Anglo-Saxons. Bede's effort itself largely defined the terms through which successive generations have understood the events of Dark Age Britain almost to our own time. The significance of Bede's reliance upon Gildas is another vital assessment of the legendary status that Gildas himself achieved.

## Bede's view of Badon: the great British victory
## from the English perspective

The Venerable Bede provides a useful counterpoint to the account of Gildas in his *Historia ecclesiastica gentis Anglorum* (History of the English Church and People), completed in 731.[18] Setting Bede in opposition to Gildas, however, is problematic in that the former drew so heavily on the latter as a source. Still, their viewpoints were radically different, and although Bede does not mention Arthur by name any more than Gildas does, he is more forthcoming on some other points, most notably in attributing, in Chapter Fifteen, the name Vortigern to the unhappy *superbus tyrannus* mentioned by Gildas as he who opened the gates of Britain to the Anglo-Saxon onslaught. Bede dates this invitation to the reign of the emperors Marcian and Valentinian, which he notes began in 449 and lasted some seven years.

As might be expected in a history of the English by an Englishman, Bede is detailed in his account of the place of origin and subsequent settlement of the Angles, Saxons and Jutes, as well as concerning the names of the chief leaders of the invaders, including a lineage dating back to Woden. In the same chapter Bede also adds the significant detail that the Angles soon entered into an alliance with the very Picts Vortigern had paid them to dispel. Perhaps unsurprisingly, Bede is quick to take up Gildas's theme of the pagan Anglo-Saxons acting as the scourge of God upon the sinful although Christian Britons, but for a somewhat different purpose, and thus in what may seem a less strident tone. Bede's focus on the function of those barbaric mercenaries as manifestations of the will of God is perhaps to be expected of a descendant of those selfsame pagan marauders.

Still, Bede compares his forebears to the Chaldeans who razed the Temple in Jerusalem, thus acting as agents of God's vengeance against the decadent Israelites; the blazes set alight by the pillaging Angles, Bede informs us, were God's just punishment upon an unrighteous British nation.[19] It is noteworthy that Bede includes another description of the sins of the Britons in Chapter 22: he notes that, even during the period of peace from external enemies that followed the events at Badon, the island of Britain was plagued by internal strife, especially once the generation which had learned the lessons of the previous scourge had passed away. Here Bede self-consciously cites Gildas as a Briton who decried the sinfulness of his own people; moreover, Bede is careful to note among the most heinous sins of the British their failure to attempt to convert the heathen invaders, a crime of particular grievousness to a churchman descended from those same pagans.

In Chapter Sixteen Bede follows the wording of Gildas fairly closely in his discussion of the successful British counter-offensive under the leadership of Ambrosius Aurelius. Bede, again taking his cue from Gildas, mentions that after this initial victory there was a certain give and take in the military engagements between the foes, culminating in a decisive – if impermanent – British victory at Mount Badon. Bede assigns to this battle a date some 44 years after the Angles arrived in Britain, which would be between 493 and 500, a date that agrees with that suggested by Gildas and others. Bede does not mention Arthur, which is unsurprising given his primary source for this information. In short, Bede, like Gildas, is perhaps most important to the student of Arthuriana in that he emphasizes periods of sin and revival among the British that are concurrent with political and military struggles. Arthur, like Ambrosius, might perhaps be described in this context as a saviour figure available to a properly penitent people. The 'Breton hope' – and associated notions later famously encapsulated as the 'once and future king' – take on a particular poignancy which perhaps achieves its mythic culmination in descriptions of Arthur's final journey to Avalon, which in archetypal terms is an apotheosis appropriate to a Christ-like saviour figure. Thus the physical location of the Battle of Mount Badon may matter less than its mythic centrality to notions of spiritual struggle and divinely mandated victory in the landscape of the Welsh psyche, becoming the shadowy source of reflections of a short-lived golden age ultimately enshrined as iconic in the British – and even in the English – sense of cultural identity. In the next chapter we will explore how gods and heroes from ancient Welsh lore likewise are recast into powerful icons of medieval British literature.

# I

# The Lost Gods
# of Avalon

A rthurian tales contain a veritable treasure trove of traditional
names, settings and stories drawn from the British mythology,
folklore and legends of yore, and in this chapter we will discover
the identities of Celtic gods and goddesses, as well as ancient heroes
and monsters disguised behind a thin veil of medieval Arthurian
lore. Welsh stories are particularly rich in this regard, and thus we
will examine closely the adventures of Owain, Peredur and Gereint,
who provide very native British faces of three Arthurian heroes
best-known through their French doppelgangers developed by
Chrétien de Troyes. We will also look at the Anglo-Norman *Lanval*,
a product of the pen of Marie de France, one of the most important
women writers of the Middle Ages. Finally, we will turn to *Sir
Gawain and the Green Knight*, one of the best-known and most
well-loved stories of the Middle Ages, seeking beneath the familiar
face of this hero and his adventure often-overlooked mythic and
folkloric attributes dating back into the mists of time. In the visages
of these Arthurian heroes, then – three Welsh, one Anglo-Norman
and one quintessentially English – we will search for glimpses of
ancient heroes and gods, figures shrouded in medieval masks which
obscure their original identities.

## Ancient Welsh faces of Arthurian heroes

### *Owain*, or 'The Lady of the Fountain': the Welsh Arthurian hero becomes the 'Knight of the Fountain'

*Owain*, also known as *Chwedyl Iarlles y Ffynnawn*, or 'The Lady of the Fountain', is one of the Welsh *Tair Rhamant*, 'Three Romances', and appears in both of the main manuscripts contained in the collection we know as the *Mabinogion*. The earliest surviving version of *Owain* is, therefore, dated from the early fourteenth century, and thus is easily 100–150 years younger than *Yvain*, the French Arthurian romance of Chrétien de Troyes with which the Welsh text is closely parallel.[1] It is possible, however, that both texts are derived from a common Welsh ancestor.[2] In any case, *Owain* is of most interest to a student of Arthurian mythology for its distinctly Welsh flavour, which is peppered with local details.[3]

Once upon a time at the court of Arthur at Caerleon, Cynon, 'Divine Hound',[4] son of Clydno, told a tale of an adventure: following the directions of a mighty one-footed black cyclops, Cynon found a fountain beside a great tree. A silver bowl was attached by a silver chain to a marble slab near the fountain. Throwing a bowlful of water from the fountain onto the slab, Cynon saw what the dark giant had foretold: a mighty hailstorm stripped leaf and life from the countryside all around, and Cynon and his horse were saved only by their armour. After the storm had passed a flock of birds roosted in the tree and sang the most delightful song Cynon had ever heard, but immediately thereafter a massive black knight on a black steed arrived, upbraided the foolish young hero for wreaking death and desolation throughout the realm, unhorsed him, and left Cynon to walk back to the court of Arthur in defeat and shame. Determined to challenge the mighty black knight himself, Owain soon retraced Cynon's steps to the fountain, where he mortally wounded the black knight, who retreated in haste to his home in a glittering city to die.

Owain followed hot on the heels of his fleeing opponent, being caught by the falling portcullis as he entered the gate behind the black knight, who was the lord of that city. Owain would have been killed there and then if it were not for the aid of a maiden named Luned, handmaid to the black knight's wife, the Lady of the Fountain; Luned gave to Owain a magic ring which made him invisible. Through the intercession of Luned, Owain eventually wooed and won the Lady of the Fountain, replacing her former consort, whom Owain had killed, and taking on that dead lord's mantle as the black knight – defending the magic fountain and the realm surrounding it from errant knights who would bring the devastation of the magic hailstorm, just as Owain himself once had. Eventually Arthur and his court came in search of Owain, who defeated each of Arthur's knights in turn in his guise as the black knight, until he and his cousin Gwalchmei recognized each other. Thereafter Owain travelled back to the Court of Arthur, but although the Lady of the Fountain had granted him leave for three months, Owain stayed with Arthur three years, until a messenger from the Lady of the Fountain sought him out at Arthur's table, reclaimed the magic ring and named him an oath-breaker.

Disconsolate, Owain left the court the next day, living as a wild man in the wastes at the edge of the world. Transformed by his life in the wilderness into an unrecognizable, hairy hermit, Owain was eventually brought back to his old self by a widow of the region, a once wealthy lady whose possessions had been seized by a greedy neighbour. After being nursed back to health, Owain borrowed arms and armour and served justice upon the enemy of his patroness, restoring to her those properties she had lost. Returning to the edge of the world, Owain came upon a pure white lion under attack by a giant serpent, which Owain slew; thereafter the lion followed Owain as faithfully as might a dog. Owain had further adventures in the wilderness, saving – with his lion's aid – the virgin daughter of a besieged lord from a lustful and flesh-eating giant, and eventually (again, with the help of his loyal lion) freeing Luned from an imprisonment brought upon her for defending Owain's honour. Eventually reconciling with the Lady of the Fountain, Owain returned with his wife to the Court of Arthur, sallying forth to defeat the evil knight known as *Du Traws*, the 'Black Oppressor'. Fulfilling the terms of a prophecy, Owain's victory in that contest transformed the hero's dark nemesis from the vicious slayer of dozens of knights and the ruthless jailer of their ladies into a hospitaller dedicated to preserving life and granting refuge and succour to the needy. Owain remained with Arthur until departing to

Albrecht Dürer, 'Sylvan Men with Heraldic Shields', 1499,
oil on lindenwood (panels flanking the *Portrait of Oswolt Krel*).

his own domain, where Owain was never defeated, as the head of the Three Hundred Swords of Cenferchyn. Nor did Owain's mystical 'Flight of Ravens' ever suffer a loss. One can learn more about this band of feathered warriors in *Breuddwyd Rhonabwy*, the 'Dream of Rhonabwy', also contained in the *Mabinogion*.[5]

Owain's transformation into a hermit in the wilderness is clearly evocative of the hermetic tradition of the Desert Fathers of the early Church – stories of whom were widely known and admired throughout the Middle Ages – but much more significant in this context is the influence of the theme of the wild hermit of the forest, widespread in Britain and derived from ancient pagan roots. Known in the Irish and Scottish traditions as the *Gruagach*, or 'Long-haired Wight', such a creature can appear either as a wild, unkempt goblin or ogre, or, alternatively, as a fairy man or woman; in either case the creature characteristically dwells alone in the forest.[6] The English equivalent is known as the *Woodwose*, or the 'Wild Man of the Wood'. In British medieval romance, this theme is perhaps most notably manifested by the eponymous hero of *Sir Orfeo*, who wanders disconsolate in the wastes after his wife is kidnapped by the fairies.

Owain's wanderings also resonate with the archetypal hero's journey through the underworld: after a first set of trials represented by his initial adventures in the Land of the Fountain, Owain undergoes a second – and far more potent – spiritual journey through his hermit-like existence in the forest. At the same time, Owain undergoes a ritual purification through a crucible of penance and suffering, culminating in his battle against the Black Oppressor. Owain's battle against the Black Oppressor represents the final step in the hero's own journey of transformation from an oath-breaker into an ideal hero.[7] He emerges from his travails transformed into a new form in which he is fit to go back to lead Arthur's war-band until he returns to his own domain; Owain lives for the rest of his life as an ideal husband to his lady. After his transformation, Owain is known as *Iarll y Cawg*, the 'Knight of the Fountain'.

The literary Owain may have had a counterpart in the person of Owain ap Urien, a sixth-century stalwart bulwark against the onslaught of the Anglo-Saxons in his father's ancient northern British domain of Rheged.[8] This region by that time had become an increasingly isolated Welsh-speaking area in the vicinity of modern-day Carlisle. Owain ap Urien was said to have won a great victory over the Anglo-Saxons around 593, and over the course of time he developed the trappings of a hero of Welsh mythology and legend: said to be a patron of the great Welsh poet Taliesin, Owain ap Urien is the subject of an elegiac work purported to be by that bard. Owain ap Urien also appears elsewhere in the Welsh Arthurian canon, notably as Arthur's opponent in *gwyddbwyll* – a Welsh chess-like game – in *Breuddwyd Rhonabwy*. In that tale, Owain has under his command his signature 'Flight', or army, of ravens, an evocative image clearly linking this figure with ancient Celtic symbols of battle, slaughter, death and the potent deities which preside over such conflicts. Perhaps most significantly, one of the Welsh Triads describes Owain ap Urien as the product of the union between his father and Modron, the early Welsh manifestation of the ancient Celtic mother goddess.[9] Thus in the figure of the legendary Owain – the seed from which the romance of *Owain* blossoms – we have both another example of the mythic hero's divine descent and an echo of the ancient Celtic rite of the ceremonial sexual union between a king and the goddess who represented life, growth and fertility in his land.

## *Peredur, Son of Efrawg*: the Welsh Grail hero on a Grail-less quest for vengeance

Like *Owain*, *Peredur* is one of the *Tair Rhamant*, or 'Three Romances', which survive in the *Mabinogion*. Like the other two great Welsh Arthurian romances, *Peredur* is both closely related to and yet distinct from its parallel tale told by Chrétien de Troyes; again, although the surviving manuscripts containing the *Tair Rhamant* were compiled considerably later than the time of Chrétien, there are solid reasons to suggest that both versions drew from older sources. Indeed, the *Annales Cambriae* mentions one Peredur, the seventh son of Eilffer, whose death is dated to AD 580.[10] In any case, *Peredur* manifests a number of medieval Welsh and even ancient Celtic characteristics that make it worthy of study in its own right. Perhaps most notable among these characteristics is the absence of the Holy Grail. The Grail – chief object of interest in the French version – is replaced in this Welsh tale by the disembodied head of Peredur's cousin. For that reason *Peredur* is often considered a Grail-less Grail tale, although the name 'Peredur' itself comes from a root which means 'bowl'.[11]

Peredur was born the seventh son of the widow of Efrawg, a name also used for the site in Britain which came to be called York.[12] Efrawg and his six older sons all perished violently, so Peredur's wise and loving mother determined to raise her remaining child in peaceful innocence, completely ignorant of the notion of chivalry and the ways of warfare. To this purpose she removed herself from the seat of power and made for an abode deep in the forest, surrounding herself and her son only with those who knew nothing of combat and were unfit for it. Peredur grew up strong and swift, with an innate nobility and a natural sense of fair play. Peredur's incredible physical prowess – coupled with his remarkable personal innocence – was illustrated one day when he came upon a herd of his mother's goats in the company of two hinds; supposing the deer to be straying goats so long wild that they had lost their horns, the boy ran down the beasts on foot. All who witnessed the fruits of Peredur's chase were amazed that anyone could manage such a feat.

Although isolated, the lad came across knights of Arthur's court and determined to become one of them, fashioning his own rustic versions of arms and armour, and leaving in search of adventure on a bony old nag from his mother's stables. Before Peredur left his mother, she offered him a number of precepts about chivalrous behaviour: he should pray at any church he came across; he should take by force food if it was not graciously offered to him; he should answer cries of distress; he should claim and distribute gems as he found them; and he should pursue fair maidens. These rules, she promised him, would make him a virtuous knight. To a sheltered innocent such as Peredur, however, such instructions seemed destined to lead to misadventure. Indeed, when Peredur claimed a kiss, a feast and a golden ring from the maiden companion of the Arrogant Knight of the Meadow, the Arrogant Knight swore vengeance, setting off in pursuit of Peredur.

At Arthur's court, Peredur was first mocked but then revered when he avenged a slight to Queen Gwenhwyfar. Peredur also vowed at the same time to wreak vengeance upon Cei, who had woefully mistreated a dwarf couple who had been the only members of the court to have greeted Peredur courteously upon his arrival. Peredur then rode forth a knight errant, vowing to send every knight he defeated to the court of Arthur. As Peredur continued his wanderings he was mentored by two lords, both his uncles: the first lame and the second the master of a hall into which a bleeding lance and a grisly platter of blood and a decapitated head were brought while Peredur was in attendance there. Since his uncle continued to speak amicably with him, however, Peredur ignored the spectacle and concomitant lamentation.

Travelling on, Peredur saved the dominion of a young virgin whose lands had been seized by a neighbouring lord. At the time of Peredur's

*Bas-de-page* miniature of Arthur riding to Mass,
with Camelot depicted as an Italian city.

arrival, the lady and her retainers were reduced to one last meal of wine and bread provided by a nearby convent. Peredur vanquished the maiden's enemies and reinstated to her the rightful possessions which had been stolen by her neighbour. Continuing his journey, Peredur soon met and overcame the Arrogant Knight of the Meadow. Peredur forced the knight to reconcile with his bride, whom the Arrogant Knight had shamed because Peredur had taken from her a kiss, a feast and a ring. Peredur then overcame the chief of the Nine Witches of Caer Loyw, who for three weeks thereafter tutored the lad in the finer points of combat. Soon after, Peredur was transfixed by the crimson, white and black of a raven feasting upon a duck in the snow; these colours reminded Peredur of the maiden he loved best, Angharad of the Golden Hand, and he fell into a reverie upon this beauty which did not lift – as the entire court of Arthur came upon him, failing to recognize him. Each of Arthur's knights challenged the wanderer, who threw down each in turn, until Gwalchmei approached Peredur courteously, and, discovering his identity, presented him to Arthur.

Returning to Caerleon with the king and his court, Peredur's affections were spurned by Angharad of the Golden Hand, and he vowed not to speak to another Christian until she accepted his suit. Thereafter Peredur defeated a lion and then a valley of treacherous giants. He also slew a mighty serpent and took from it a golden ring. Peredur travelled far and wide as 'the Mute Warrior', transformed in visage due to his lovesickness, finally winning the love of Angharad and henceforth being able to speak again. Peredur continued to seek honour thereafter, defeating the one-eyed Dark Oppressor and learning from that opponent the journey necessary to face the Black Worm of the Barrow, which was hidden within the Sorrowful Mound.

This quest took Peredur through the domain of the King of Suffering, to the court of the Lady of Feats, and finally to the Sorrowful Mound itself. Along the way, Peredur saw many wonders, such as the daily reviving of the three sons of the King of Suffering in a tub of warm water after they were slain each day by the fearsome Addanc, a lake monster. Peredur met atop a mound the fairest of all maidens, who sought to save his life by giving him a magic stone which would render him invisible. He also came across two herds of magical colour-changing sheep and a tree that blazed in flame on one side and yet was green and verdant on the other. Cresting a nearby mound Peredur met a hunting lord who tried to dissuade the hero from his path, but the young knight did not rest until he had slain and decapitated the Addanc. Peredur then sought the Black Worm of the Sorrowful Mound, defeating in a series of single combats a horde of heroes who had gathered to attempt the same feat. He slew the Black Worm and took its priceless treasure, which he gave to his loyal retainer Etlym Gleddyf Coch, whose name means 'Blade of Crimson'.

Peredur next won a great tournament in a vale of watermills and windmills, becoming therefore the 'Knight of the Mill', and winning the right to become consort to the Empress of Constantinople, none other than the maiden on the mound who had given him the magic stone, and with whom he now sojourned for fourteen years. One day, when Peredur was again with Arthur, a horrible, hideous old hag entered the court and berated Peredur for his silence in the court of his uncle the Fisher King, when the young knight had failed to investigate the bleeding lance, the bloody salver or his uncle's lameness. During the course of his quest to learn more, the hag – known as the Dark Maiden – became a mystical guide of sorts as Peredur visited the Castle of Wonders, found and threw away a magical *gwyddbwyll* board (a chess-like game), met and defeated the Swart Warrior, and hunted and slew the one-horned stag. Finally, the Dark Maiden was revealed to be a magically transformed squire, Peredur's own cousin, who revealed to him the meaning of the secrets of the Lame Lord.

The disembodied head belonged to another of Peredur's cousins. He had been slain by the witches of Caer Loyw, whose chief Peredur had once defeated, and that coven was also responsible for the laming of Peredur's uncle. A prophecy foretold, the boy continued, that Peredur would avenge these evils. In the company of Arthur and his men, Peredur descended upon the witches of Caer Loyw. During the battle Peredur brought his blade down upon the crown of one hag so that her helmet, head and armour were shorn in two. With her dying cry that witch called upon her sisters to fly, as the man they had trained in arms was returned, and a prophecy had foretold their doom at his hands. Thus were the witches of Caer Loyw slain, and thus was the evil they had wrought upon Peredur's uncle and cousin avenged.

Peredur's vow of silence to all Christians until he wins the heart of Angharad – a name one could read as 'Most Beloved One' – might be said to represent the young hero's quest for true love. His subsequent adventures, however, also give rise to an opportunity for that hero to engage in a series of archetypal battles with monsters, in this case a lion, a race of giants and a huge serpent. While the lion and the serpent reflect rather standard obstacles, the giants provide a more intriguing opportunity for mythic analysis. These giants, who it is clear in the text are pagan, never allow a Christian to escape alive from their valley; Peredur defeats a great many of them in combat, and then grants the survivors quarter provided that they accept baptism, submit to the sovereignty of Arthur and report that they were vanquished by Peredur. In addition to the standard hero's conflict with monstrous foes, then, this adventure comprises a spiritual as well as a physical battle; indeed, the core of this episode seems to emanate from the tradition of saints' lives and conversion narratives as much as from epic heroic roots. Here we are provided with a glimpse of how the medieval Welsh tradition might have transformed a tribe of figures from an earlier age, just as medieval Irish mythology relegated to the world under the green hillocks of Ireland its previous waves of invaders – as well as gods and demons of the pre-Christian traditions – who are recast as powerful but non-divine other races.

Although the giants that Peredur subdues might indeed be identified as such by their gargantuan size, they are only identified as evil enemies when their secret plans are revealed: the daughter of their chief informs the young hero of the nature of his hosts' intentions. This altogether scurrilous band of wretches greeted their visitor in friendship but planned to slay him without mercy at sunrise. This description of such dangerous and despicable 'others' may spring from a number of possible sources. Such details suggest a common primal fear of generically barbarous alien tribes and their deceitful ways. More chillingly, the threat of isolated pockets of pagan clans who slay – perhaps for sacrificial or cannibalistic rituals – Christian visitors also might represent a distant echo of anxieties rooted in perceived historical realities: isolated pagan hill-folk might be reputed to be cannibals. It is perhaps of particular note that secrecy from and security against the outside Christian world seems to be a paramount concern of this race of outliers, as is manifested by the hidden nature of their valley and its carefully protected access. Moreover, in these brutal false friends bent on his destruction it is possible that the medieval Welsh hero Peredur faces faint reflections of ancient mythic figures of bygone pagan traditions; indeed, the mighty ones from the past might well appear writ large in medieval texts because of their immense powers of old, just as the Arthur of yore appears as a giant in *Breuddwyd Rhonabwy*, towering above his lesser visitor from latter days.

Peredur's recapture of the lost holdings of a maiden beset by a domineering neighbour manifests a common romance motif seen – to cite but one obvious example – in Owain's similar victory over the dastardly neighbouring lord who thought to take by force the lady who nursed Owain after his sojourn in the wilderness. Moreover, the heiress maiden whose dominion is saved for her by Peredur also evokes the familiar Celtic theme of the tripartite colours of the true love with her white flesh, rosy cheeks and black brows and hair; in addition, the meal provided to her court by the convent evokes the Last Supper, and Peredur's role in sharing out all of the portions thereof equally underscores his identity as a Christ-like figure.

The beautiful lady who appears to Peredur atop the mound prophesies his doom and in return for his love offers him a magical stone which will allow him to vanquish the Addanc. She recalls any number of women with supernatural powers, often of fairy origin. In the context of the Welsh tradition, however, the clearest parallel is probably with Rhiannon, that euhemerized Celtic horse goddess whom Pwyll spies from the top of the enchanted mound and eventually takes as his wife. In any case, such a mound is often construed as a boundary or portal between the ordinary world of humans and the otherworld populated by supernatural creatures, gods and fairies. Furthermore, Peredur's adventure in the Addanc's cave is marked as the archetypal hero's journey to the underworld in other ways as well. The fact that each son of the King of Suffering goes every day to die in the otherworldly lair of the monster only to have his corpse resurrected at the hand of a beloved lady in the land of the living underscores the division between the domain of the powers of death and destruction and that of the powers of life and love. Moreover, in the sounds of the hunting pack with which the lord attempts to waylay Peredur we might hear distant echoes of the *cwn annwfn*, the great 'hell hounds' of Welsh mythology led by the infernal huntsman Gwyn ap Nudd. Also, the river in the valley clearly demarks a boundary between worlds which the sheep can navigate, changing colour as they move from one world to the next. Finally, the signal tree – one half of which eternally blazes from its tip to its root and the other half of which blossoms evergreen – is a rather obvious boundary marker, and just beyond it Peredur meets the fairy lord who directs him to the lair of the Addanc of the Lake, which in this case is no less than a manifestation of death itself; moreover the Addanc – although clearly called a resident of a lake and notably drawn from a Welsh tradition of water monsters – is specifically anthropomorphized into a spectre of a death god, complete with a missile of death.[13] Indeed, this creature is specifically said to reside in a cave, which in itself makes reference to an ancient Celtic commonplace concerning portals to the otherworld. The tub in which the lifeless corpses of the sons of the King of Suffering are revived each day clearly brings to mind the theme of the Cauldron of Life, which is most famously evoked in the Second Branch of the *Mabinogion*, in which dead warriors are resurrected. It is also worth noting that magic cauldrons are often associated with the otherworld in the Welsh tradition.

The hero's fourteen-year liaison with the Empress of Constantinople is of particular note because this episode is certainly absent from Chrétien de Troyes' version of the adventures of the Grail hero, and thus illuminates a peculiarly Welsh aspect of the tale of Peredur which distinguishes it from that of Perceval. The empress is also the fairy-like woman who appeared to Peredur on a mound as he made his way to do battle with the Addanc of the Lake. Thus the Empress is at one and the same time an otherworldly feminine spirit with wide-ranging powers which allow her to appear and disappear at will, travel immense distances and offer the hero magical aid and protection in his battle with the serpent-demon Addanc, an icon of death itself; as such, this lady is clearly representative of the ancient Celtic Sovranty ('Sovereignty') figure. This iconic status is underscored by her later identification as the Empress of Constantinople, the ruler of the most powerful city and empire in the medieval European imagination. The detail that Peredur co-rules with this feminine personification of political power seems, in this context, a distant echo of the ancient Celtic mythological rite of passage through which a king established his right to rule through union with the goddess representing the land he sought to govern.

Peredur's hunt for the one-horned stag combines the general medieval theme of the pestilent beast with the traditional Celtic fascination with the stag; Peredur's conflict with this creature also provides another prime example of this hero's archetypal battles with monsters, as well as resonance with the ancient Celtic god Cernunnos and the British hunt god Cocidius. The antlers of the horned god and his totemic beasts are phallic images all the more fantastic and appropriate because of the hardness of the horn; indeed, antlers were often used to create charms and talismans, carved into overtly phallic forms. The single antler of the one-horned stag serves to emphasize this association; here a symbol of fertility seems to be inverted, and the one-horned stag – according to the Dark Maiden's account – has literally starved the forest of its vitality in order to draw all of the life force unto itself.

The one-horned stag evokes the ancient bounty we might expect to be associated with such a figure drawn from the Celtic tradition. The slain stag's head, meanwhile, therefore represents both a champion's portion and trophy – as does the stag's head awarded to Gereint, son of Erbin, in his own tale – as well as the capture of the potency which the beast symbolized in life. The golden torc about the neck of the One Horned Stag, meanwhile, recalls the sacred torc so often associated with the figure of Cernunnos, the horned god of the Celts.

It is also noteworthy that the stalking of stags commonly results in transcending the borders with the otherworld in medieval Irish and Welsh literature. This trope is nowhere more common than in the *Mabinogion* proper, and it is in such a context that Pwyll, for example, stumbles into Annwfn in the First Branch. The Dark Maiden's claim that no mortal had dared to enter the forest of the one-horned stag for a year might serve to support the idea that this region comprises a borderland with the otherworld. It is also noteworthy, in such a context, that when the hero journeys to the otherworld and slays a beast there, he encounters the empress,

ₜ **Delegūrāmgouſſeheūēorlen**
**dounₐ il·⅃·rₐſiel·**

ₐ **Dₐmefₐirlₐdemoi**
**fiₑleiouuousₐpozdꝝ**

Detail of a miniature showing a damsel bringing news to Arthur and Guinevere.

who, as we have seen, is clearly more than mortal and accustomed to permeating such borders.

The description of the hag who berates Peredur before the court of Arthur is highly detailed, and this focus upon her ugliness and horrible physical attributes calls to mind a number of texts containing episodes associated with the 'Loathly Lady' tradition, including Chaucer's *Wife of Bath's Tale* and some Arthurian romances concerned with Gawain, perhaps even *Sir Gawain and the Green Knight*. The closest parallel, however, is to be found in the Middle English romance commonly known as *The Weddyng of Syr Gawen and Dame Ragnell*.[14] In brief, this tale relates how a hideous old crone saves the life of Arthur by giving him the answer to a riddle, then demands in recompense to be married to Gawain, who submits to this condition. On their wedding night, however, the woman takes on the form of a beautiful young maiden, and offers her new husband the choice of having her be lovely in public but ugly in private or vice versa; when Gawain submits to his wife's authority by allowing her to choose, she informs him that she will ever after be beautiful all the time.[15] A key theme in these tales is exactly such an act of submission. The Loathly Lady echoes ancient tripartite conceptions of Celtic goddesses, who were often rendered in the three stages of womanhood: Virgin, Wife and Crone.

In many of the texts in which the Loathly Lady theme asserts itself, the husband's submission to such a wife might be thought to evoke on some level the Sovranty theme, that is, the folkloric notion of a union between a lord and his land. Peredur's absolute obedience to the series of tasks set for him by this disguised and disagreeable mentor is reminiscent of the protagonist's submission to the Loathly Lady, and culminates in the hero's successful quest for vengeance for his decapitated cousin and lamed uncle. More to the point, it is only under the auspices of his cousin in the role of this shape-shifting shaman guide that Peredur develops an understanding of what he has seen. Before he fell under the tutelage of this Loathly Lady, Peredur's hallmark was his naivety; he was unable to comprehend the significance of what he had witnessed, and therefore the time was not yet ripe for him to avenge his kinsmen, as had been foretold. Indeed, it is only through this dawning comprehension that the hero is able to seek and claim such vengeance, and thus it is precisely the hero's journey from ignorance to clarity which is the ultimate object in the Welsh tale of the Grail-less Grail Hero.

A recurring theme is that of the young maiden offered in marriage to Peredur who loves him best of all men in the world. It is also significant that such young women offer Peredur weapons. In this repetitive formula we see the hero marked out several times as special. Indeed, given the resonance between the figure of the magical Empress of Constantinople in this medieval Welsh text and the Sovranty figure of ancient Celtic mythology, it seems clear that this romance hero is again and again anointed with the favour of a powerful feminine embodiment of martial prowess. In the context of Peredur's tutelage in the arts of war under the Witches of Caer Loyw, it seems clear that the Welsh manifestation of the Grail hero is heavily steeped in an age-old Celtic sensibility concerning the role of the war goddess in choosing the greatest hero on whom to bestow her favours.

## *Gereint fab Erbin*: the Welsh Arthurian hero as jealous lover of Lady Sovranty

Another of the *Tair Rhamant, Gereint fab Erbin* survives in a number of sources, including the manuscripts containing the *Mabinogion*. This romance recounts the love affair and adventures of Gereint and Enid, best known to students of Arthuriana through their analogues in Chrétien de Troyes' *Erec et Enide*. Like the other tales of the *Tair Rhamant*, the extant manuscript tradition of the Welsh version of this tale is considerably younger than its French counterpart, although it is highly probable that both versions draw upon an older original.[16] In this case, however, it is possible that Chrétien's version may be closer to its source, especially given the fact that Guerec is the Breton form of Erec, which may suggest that this was originally a hero of Breton provenance.[17] Breton origin might suggest that the Welsh Gereint may be the descendent of an ancient Celtic hero.

It was for many years King Arthur's custom to hold court at Caerleon on Usk, and one year, on the Tuesday after Whitsunday, a young forester appeared in that court from the Forest of Dean. The lad reported the sighting of a marvellous white stag, the most wondrous and noble creature he had ever seen. Arthur immediately resolved to go hunting for the beast with his retainers at the break of dawn; Queen Gwenhwyfar begged leave to go forth to observe the hunt, while Gwalchmei asked that whosoever was to take the white stag in the hunt might be allowed to take its head to present to a lady of his choosing.

The next morning both the queen and Gereint overslept, and rushed after the hunting party together, in the company of one of Gwenhwyfar's maidens. Along the way they encountered a mighty knight and a maiden upon a white horse, preceded by a dwarf with a flail who whipped the queen's companion. Although unarmoured, Gereint pursued this rude trio while the queen and her maiden sought the king's party. Following the dwarf and his companions, Gereint soon found himself in a city preparing for a great tournament. Seeking lodging and armour to borrow, Gereint found himself in the once great but now decayed manor of an old gentleman named Yniwl Iarll. This man had once been the lord of the region, but had been overthrown by his nephew and now lived in squalor with his wife and lovely daughter, Enid. Accepting lodging and a loan of armour from Yniwl, Gereint entered the tournament of the town and in the end challenged the champion, the same knight whose dwarf had humiliated the queen. Ultimately victorious, as the new champion Gereint took from his opponent the title 'the Knight of the Sparrowhawk', and proclaimed Enid, his lady love, the fairest at the tournament. The discourteous knight, his maiden and their dwarf were dispatched to seek the forgiveness of Gwenhwyfar. Gereint reconciled Yniwl and his nephew, and the old lord regained his lost property. Gereint left the next day with Enid, dressed only in the shift in which he had met her, to receive wedding clothes from the queen and to be given in marriage to Gereint by the king. Arthur, meanwhile, slew the white stag, which had been flushed from its cover by Cafal, the king's favourite hound. The queen then informed the court of Gereint's quest, and all agreed that the awarding of the head of the white stag should wait until Gereint returned.

The following day the broken knight defeated by Gereint, Edern Son of Nudd, appeared with his maiden and dwarf to tell of Gereint's victory and to beg the queen's forgiveness. The next day Gereint and Enid arrived to much rejoicing, and the maiden was arrayed by the queen and given in marriage to Gereint. Enid was granted the head of the white stag by Arthur, and for the next three years her reputation grew, as did Gereint's martial prowess. Then Gereint returned to his own dominion in Cornwall, taking over for his failing father, Erbin Son of Custennin. At first Gereint continued to burnish his reputation, but after a time he began to spend more time in lovemaking with his wife than in battle, and eventually word of this came to Erbin, who confronted Enid. Later hearing – only half awake and in part – Enid's lament for his loss of honour, Gereint mistakenly thought she yearned for another man. Enraged and humiliated, Gereint went wandering again, with Enid in her simple shift riding before him, commanded to remain ever silent, regardless of the danger, unless he first spoke to her.

They encountered a number of groups of knights in this manner, and although forbidden to speak, each time Enid warned her husband, who only became angered at her disobedience. Soon Enid drove before her the horses and armour of a dozen defeated knights, while Gereint followed behind. Soon after, a lord besotted with Enid attempted to woo her away from Gereint, whom Enid managed to warn. Again angered by what he perceived as her disobedience, Gereint soundly defeated the pursuing lord and his men.

As they continued their travels, Gereint and Enid came to the most beautiful valley ever seen by man. As they continued down the road into this domain they encountered a knight who warned them that it was the custom of the local lord, known as Y Brenhin Bychan, or 'the Little King', that no warrior might cross the bridge into that land without meeting the master of that demesne. Ignoring this admonition, the knight and lady continued on their way, crossing the bridge but bypassing the town. When the trespasser into Y Brenhin Bychan's territory refused to pay proper homage to him, Y Brenhin Bychan attacked, and it was soon clear that he was a doughty warrior. Moreover, in addition to the great blows he rained down upon his opponent, the tiny warrior was remarkably hard to see or hit in the midst of combat, so that it took all of Gereint's skill to defeat his assailant, to whom he granted quarter.

Gereint and Enid continued on their road into a forest after the battle with Y Brenhin Bychan, but the warrior's wounds were so great that he had to pause under the shade of a tree to rest. Enid dismounted under a different tree. Suddenly the woods rang out with the sounds of horns; it was the court of Arthur, and Gereint was determined to avoid all contact with that party. As he stood under the tree considering what he should do, however, he was spied by a servant of the king's steward, Cei, who returned to his master to report what he had seen. Cei armed himself and mounted his horse to go in search of the wounded warrior. When Cei approached the knight under the tree, he did not recognize him, although Gereint knew Cei. The steward then demanded the knight's name, or – barring that – that this knight accompany him into the presence of the king.

When the stranger refused, Cei sought to compel him, but was himself quickly thrown from his horse, although Gereint sought to do no worse to King Arthur's steward. Cei fled the scene of his humiliation in haste until he came upon Gwalchmei, whom he sent to seek this troublesome traveller. When Gwalchmei came upon Gereint he also failed to recognize his friend, and soon found himself in combat with the stranger. Suddenly perceiving the identity of this unknown knight, however, Gwalchmei called Gereint by name, and although the warrior denied his identity, Gwalchmei also saw Enid watching nearby. Appalled by the terrible wounds apparent upon his friend, Gwalchmei once more attempted to entice the bloodied knight to come to the camp of the king. When Gereint clearly refused to come to Arthur, however, Gwalchmei devised a ruse whereby the king moved his tent to the very edge of the road Gereint proposed to follow, and in this way lured his unsuspecting comrade to the court of King Arthur and the care of the royal physicians.

Once healed of his wounds, Gereint again went on his way with Enid – sworn to silence – leading him. After they had travelled some distance, they heard a blood-curdling scream. Commanding Enid to wait for him where they were, Gereint advanced to find the source of this terrible cry. A little way off he found two horses standing by the mangled corpse of a knight, with a maiden lamenting over him. The young woman related that her beloved had been slain by three giants, who afterwards had lumbered off down the high road.

Telling the maiden to go back to where Enid was and await his return, Gereint rode hard after the gargantuan marauders, whom he found not too far off. Each of the three giants was the size of three men, and each carried a huge cudgel. Spurring his horses towards the giants, Gereint managed to slay two with his lance before the third brought home a blow upon his shield, shivering it and shattering his shoulder so forcefully that all of the knight's old wounds reopened and his blood flowed forth in a great stream. With the very last of his strength Gereint drew his sword and brought down upon the last giant's head such a mighty blow that the fiend was cloven from the peak of his pate to the base of his neck. Tottering back to Enid, Gereint collapsed on the ground before his lady, who uttered a horrible wail.

In spite of Gereint's wounds, they followed the road away from that place as quickly as they could. Soon, however, they noticed behind them a great gathering of spears pursuing and gaining on them quickly. After first putting Enid safely on the other side of the hedge lining the road, Gereint turned to face those who were following them, steeling himself for conflict. The party in their wake turned out to be none other than the Little King, however, at the head of his army, come to aid, succour and lend support to Gereint, as per his vow. Taking the wounded knight to his kinsman's court, the Little King oversaw Gereint's rehabilitation under the care of the finest physicians. After six weeks Gereint was hale and whole again, and his armour had been completely refurbished. However, although Y Brenhin Bychan pressed Gereint to come to his court, the wandering knight wished to spend one more day in search of adventure, a boon to which the Little King gladly assented.

Accordingly, the next day Gereint, Enid and Y Brenhin Bychan set forth, and the lady's spirits were higher in this journey than they had been since she and her knight first set forth from their home. As they rode along the path they came to a fork, from one branch of which they met a traveller on foot. This man advised them to take the higher road, as no man had ever returned from a journey down the lower fork. This, he said, led to the Hedge of Mist, within which knights vied in magical contests; not one such contestant had ever returned alive. If the party was to continue down the low road to the Hedge of Mist, their informant continued, they would find the court of Lord Ywein, upon whom all visitors were impelled to attend. Gereint and his party determined to take the low road in spite of this warning, however, and soon found themselves courteously received and entertained at the court of Lord Ywein.

When he looked about the nobility of Gereint the lord mourned that he had ever instituted the practice of the contests within the hedge, and would have excused his guest or discontinued the ritual at a word from that warrior. Gereint, however, was not to be satisfied until he had tried his courage in that crucible, and soon after eating the knight armed himself and the company approached the Hedge of Mist. This barrier stretched up into the firmament as high as they could see, and everywhere along it sprouted a multitude of stakes, all but two of which were mounted by the grisly heads of those knights who had dared to breach the hedge.

Moving fearlessly and alone through the wall of fog until he had cleared the Hedge of Mist and discovered himself in the midst of an orchard, Gereint found a clearing in the centre of the orchard and a tent in the middle of that clearing. The door of the tent stood open, and hard by that door stood a solitary apple tree, from the branches of which hung a great hunting horn. Entering the tent, Gereint found a maiden seated on a throne of gold; the tent was otherwise empty except for another chair. When he sat upon that chair the maiden warned Gereint that the knight who owned it never suffered another to take his seat, and indeed, the young warrior had hardly uttered his disinclination to vacate the throne before the knight in question appeared at the door of the tent and challenged him to combat.

The battle between the combatants was bitter and fierce, but finally Gereint threw his opponent to the ground violently and drew his sword to take the knight's head, just as all the knight's challengers had heretofore been taken as trophies and displayed on the stakes throughout the Hedge of Mist. Before Gereint accomplished his intention, however, his defeated antagonist begged for quarter. To this piteous request Gereint assented, so long as the felled knight might cause the Hedge of Mist to lift, the contest within it never to have been, and all the related sorcery and enchantment to be undone in such a way as though they had never existed.

To all these conditions the knight agreed, informing Gereint that all that had ever been needed to undo that evil was for a valiant hero such as himself to defeat the Knight of the Garden, to take the hunting horn from the apple tree and to sound that horn; at the very moment of this clamour the Hedge of Mist would rise and be no more. It was just as the knight had said: as Enid and her companions waited anxiously for Gereint to return, suddenly the hunting horn sounded from the depths of the garden and the Hedge of Mist lifted and was gone forever. Then all present were reconciled with one another, and not least Gereint and Enid, who soon thereafter returned to their kingdom which waxed in prosperity from that point on, just as did Gereint's prowess and valour and Enid's fame and honour.

The ranks of the heroes, foes and monsters of *Gereint fab Erbin* abound with mythic, folkloric and legendary symbolism. One figure of substantial folkloric and mythic significance, for example, is the

Sparrowhawk Knight, who is revealed to be Edern mab Nudd; Edern of Brittany, a non-canonical Breton saint, is most popular in the region of Finistère, 'Land's End', an area still rich with Breton language and folklore, as well as huge dolmens and other ancient stone monuments.[18] *Mab Nudd*, of course, implies that Edern is descended from the god of that name. The figure in this tale, then, combines the identity of a Christian pseudo-saint with that of the scion of an ancient Celtic god. In this context it is worthwhile to note that when Gwenhwyfar and Gereint first encounter Edern, their principle impression of him concerns his gigantic size; again, just like Arthur and his knights of the Dream of Rhonabwy, the gods and heroes of ancient times are writ large as giants when they reappear in medieval texts. Edern is mentioned in a number of other Welsh Arthurian texts as well, including *Culhwch ac Olwen* and *Breuddwyd Rhonabwy*. Later Arthurian manifestations of Edern, it has been suggested, may include Isdernus, Ydier filz Nu, Hilderus and Yder de Northumbie.

Y Brenhin Bychan, known in French as Gwiffred Petit, or the 'Little King', is one of the most interesting figures in this tale, clearly meant to evoke one of those who have come to be called the 'Little People', the magical dwarves or elves often known to later folklore as fairies. It is clear from the actions of Edern mab Nudd's small but vile companion earlier in this same text that dwarves in medieval Welsh literature need not be magical nor good. In the case of Y Brenhin Bychan, however, who is identified as the lord of the fairest of all domains, it seems equally clear that they certainly may be. It is perhaps of particular note that the Little King who appears in the Welsh tale of Gereint is not first and foremost referred to as a dwarf, although he is clearly understood to be very, very small. It may be that we have here a conflation of the medieval Celtic tradition of little folk – who are often stunted versions of ancient Celtic deities – with the common medieval romance motif of the fairies as inhumanly beautiful creatures who inhabit an otherworld much more wonderful than our own.

Giants, at the other end of the otherworldly spectrum, provide another classic mythological foe for this hero, who confronts these huge adversaries courageously and successfully, although he himself just barely survives the encounter. The death-swoon into which

Gereint falls at Enid's feet, moreover, provides a mythologically tinged plot device whereby the estranged lovers are reconciled, culminating in a sort of romance hero's journey to the underworld from which the protagonist emerges with new, clearer vision and understanding concerning his lady's love for him. As far as the earl's men are concerned, Gereint rises from the embrace of death itself to save his lady; he seems to be brought back from the brink of the abyss only by the keening wail of Enid, his one true love. Indeed, it is only after this deathbed conversion that Gereint understands how completely he has misinterpreted Enid's affection for him and how vilely he has wronged her.

Enid herself is a figure of some significant mythological and folkloric valence. The name 'Enid' may be rendered something like 'Life Force', so it is perhaps not terribly surprising that Gereint finds it difficult to depart from his lady's bed, and that he loses interest in all other pursuits. Indeed, given the context of the Sovranty theme which reasserts itself throughout the *Tair Rhamant*, this sequence of events is all the more significant: it is much more than the mere romance motif of a lover's inappropriate attachment to the object of his desire which it may at first glance appear. Ancient Celtic mythology and ritual is steeped in the tradition of the warrior king whose rule is predicated upon his relationship with some form or other of the fertility goddess, and medieval Welsh and Irish tales which draw upon these traditions are legion. In this light, even the stipulation that every knight who would contend for the sparrowhawk must appear with his one true lady love might suggest a mythic subtext for a common-enough romance convention.

It is also noteworthy in such a context that the warrior hero of this tale refuses to consummate his relationship with the virginal figure representing the fertility goddess except by the highest authority. Gereint will only take Enid from the hands of Arthur and Gwenhwyfar in person; indeed, the marriage bed in which Gereint consummates his union with Enid is placed in the very bedchamber of the king and queen. The fact that soon after their union Enid, she of the highest reputation in all of Britain, receives the head of the white stag – with all of the associations of fertility manifested by the king of the forest's antlers, which moreover provide the fundamental emblem of Cernunnos, the horned god of Celtic mythology – further emphasizes her identity as a fertility figure. That Enid reflects ancient attributes of Lady Sovranty may be inferred, in addition, by the fact that Gereint succeeds to his own kingdom shortly after consummating his union with her. Although his prowess and fame grow after this consummation, eventually he becomes besotted with his mate. After all, the allure of such a goddess is undeniable, and thus Gereint's irresistible attraction to Enid makes all the more sense. Such a relationship has responsibilities as well as pleasures, however, and the chosen champion must practice the arts of war as well as those of love.

The lineage of Gereint himself is rich in folkloric, mythic and even legendary progenitors. The name 'Gereint' is generally agreed to have originated in the earlier Latinized form 'Gerontius', the name of at least one Roman general in fifth-century Britain. A number of

Tintagel Passage is of uncertain date and unknown function. Possibly once used as a cellar, it seems to have involved the extension of an existing cave.

members of British ruling families subsequently carried variations of such a name. Concerning the most significant of these, the specific figure of Gereint fab Erbin is thought to have been derived in some part from an actual king of Dumnonia, a realm situated in the area of present-day Devon and Cornwall. This same Gereint himself ruled from Tintagel and is thought to have perished in the closing decades of the sixth century; his notoriety was such that he may be referenced in *Y Gododdin*.[19] In the Arthurian canon this figure is sometimes cited as a close kinsman and contemporary of Arthur, perhaps because a nobleman by the name of Gerontius was said to have fought against the Anglo-Saxon invaders in a great battle around the year 500. This conflict was the subject of a contemporary poem, which was itself the source of another text – several hundred years later – which renamed this hero as Gereint, and which mentioned the presence of the men of Arthur at the battle in question. Such confusion is also the result of the fact that a certain Gereint is said to have been the father of Cadwy, a contemporary of Arthur's who appears as a scion of the ruling house of Dumnonia in the *Vita Sancti Carantoci Prima*; this same figure is also known through Geoffrey of Monmouth as Cador.[20] The name Gereint has also been linked with that of Gerennius of Cornwall, a folkloric hero who is closely associated with the Cornish hillfort at Dingerein, and who lends his name to the nearby site of Gerrans. In any case, in the Gereint of the *Mabinogion* we find a hero with an ancient British pedigree, and who is a suitable warrior-consort for Enid, the medieval daughter of an equally venerable Celtic Sovranty goddess.

## The folkloric Norman-French face of an Arthurian hero

Marie de France is generally cited as the first major woman writer of the Middle Ages, and she has been argued to have been the finest medieval writer of short tales before Boccaccio and Chaucer. Although Marie lived in England and wrote for the English court, her name suggests that she was French by birth. Some have suggested that Marie may have been an illegitimate sister to Henry II and abbess of Shaftesbury; it is certain, in any case, that she was a noble woman, possibly of religious vocation, and she certainly seems to

Marie de France writing; an illumination from a late 13th-century
French manuscript.

have had courtly connections. Marie de France composed her stories
in the second half of the twelfth century. These are in the form of
short tales full of folkloric material thought to have possibly originated in lyric form in Brittany, and hence they are called 'Breton lais'.[21]
Marie wrote in the Anglo-Norman French dialect used at the court
of Henry ii of England, who reigned from 1154 to 1189.

In addition to the lais, Marie penned a collection of animal fables,
as well as *St Patrick's Purgatory*. The complete collection of the lais
of Marie de France, twelve in all, is found only in a single manuscript
from the mid-thirteenth century now housed in the British Museum;
a slightly later manuscript, containing a collection of nine of these
lais in another order, resides in the Bibliothèque Nationale in Paris.
A lone lai or fragment has been found in each of three other manuscripts of the thirteenth and fourteenth centuries. The lai of Marie
de France of most interest to students of Arthuriana is *Lanval*, which
recounts the travails of a mortal knight from the court of King Arthur
who becomes the lover of a fairy maiden.

## *Lanval*: the Arthurian hero takes a fairy lover

*Lanval* concerns the story of a knight of that name who wins the secret love of a fairy maiden, only to lose her because of the intrigues of Queen Guinevere. The true love of Lanval and his lady eventually overcomes the resentful envy of the queen, although only in the nick of time. The explicit mythic context of the descriptions of the power and majesty of Lanval's fairy lover, as well as the superiority of the otherworld she inhabits, are of particular interest to those interested in Arthurian mythology.

This story is retold a number of times throughout the Middle Ages, notably in the late fourteenth-century Middle English romance *Sir Launfal*, by Thomas Chestre.[22] For his primary source Chestre drew upon *Sir Landeval*, which was composed by an unknown hand some half a century earlier. Although the anonymous author of *Sir Landeval* does not seem to have utilized the work of Marie de France directly, the evidence suggests that the ultimate origin of *Sir Landeval* was either a source used by Marie or else a Middle English redaction of her own *Lanval*. Whatever the case, *Sir Landeval* seems to have shared its ur-source with two works evoking similar themes, *Sir Lambewell* and *Sir Lamwell*, which both date from around two centuries later than *Sir Landeval*.

Lanval was a knight who had served Arthur well, although when the time came to give gifts of wealth and wives to his followers, the king forgot this one loyal retainer. Many in the king's court were jealous of Lanval, of his courage and his beauty and his largess; indeed, many envious men who claimed friendship to Lanval's face secretly took joy in his struggles. Although he was the son of a mighty and powerful king, the prince was far from home. Lanval, although attached to the king's own household, thus found himself friendless. He had spent all his money, but was too proud to approach the king; nor did his lord offer him any assistance.

Wandering in the countryside one day to lament his woes, Lanval came across the most beautiful maiden in the world in the richest and most costly pavilion. The lady declared her love for Lanval, they consummated that love, and after an afternoon of bliss she sent him off with untold riches and the promise to appear to him privately whenever he desired her. The lady's only condition was that Lanval never, under any circumstances, speak of her to any mortal, lest he forfeit her, her love and her gifts ever after. From that moment on, Lanval and all his household were the most richly appointed at court, and Lanval was exceedingly generous to all. Nothing gave him more pleasure than largess, except for the pleasure of his lady's company, which he enjoyed privately as often as possible. Because of his wealth, nobility and generosity, Lanval again came to the attention of the court, and one day was invited by Gawain to join with the others at sport. As Lanval sat a little apart, contemplating the memory of his lady love, the queen was drawn to him and propositioned him; aghast, Lanval refused to betray Arthur. The queen then accused Lanval of preferring young boys to women. Stung, Lanval retorted that even the lowliest of her serving girls was more comely than the queen, thus insulting Guinevere and breaking his vow at the same time.

Furious, the queen claimed that Lanval had attempted to thrust himself upon her, and had insulted her beauty when she refused him. Enraged, the king sentenced Lanval to death unless he could prove his claim of his lady's surpassing beauty. Lanval, meanwhile, distraught by the fact that he had lost his love by breaking his vow, didn't care whether he lived or died. Condemned to be tried before a jury of his peers, Lanval was released on the bond provided by Gawain and other nobles who now recognized his worth. Since he only might be acquitted if his lady were to appear before the court, unfortunately, Lanval despaired. On the day of his trial, however, the proceedings were interrupted a number of times by progressively more beautiful maidens announcing that their lady was to visit the court, and asking Arthur to render his hall fit for their mistress. Finally, the lady herself arrived, and all agreed that she was the most beautiful in all the world. She rode a snow-white steed with tack and harness worth a king's ransom, with a sparrowhawk upon her arm and a greyhound in her wake. Before her came a page with an ivory horn. The lady declared that Guinevere's accusations were false, and her beauty itself proved the truth of Lanval's boast. Acquitted, Lanval leapt from the mounting block in the courtyard onto the back of his lady's horse, encircling his love with his arms. According to Breton lore, Lanval travelled with his lady to Avalon, from whence he never returned.

The ivory horn carried by the page preceding Lanval's beloved certainly could be construed as a fertility symbol; furthermore, we might well take this object to be a hunting horn in the context of the sparrowhawk and the greyhound which accompany the lady. This hunting theme evokes the 'wild hunt' as it is manifested by the fairies of medieval British myth and folklore, as it is, for example, in the Middle English romance *Sir Orfeo*. Indeed, the very fact that this fairy lady first 'captured' Lanval in the midst of the day as he rested – and perhaps slumbered – by the side of the stream suggests a parallel with the noontime hunt of the fairy king in the story of Orfeo. Lanval himself does not know at first whether to believe that he met his love in a dream or in reality, and thus this first meeting resonates quite closely with the first meeting of Lady Heurodis with the king of the fairies in *Sir Orfeo*, an analogous situation further emphasized by the fact that, in the end, the fairy lady takes Lanval away from the midst of Arthur's court, never to return, just as the fairy king did to

Detail of a miniature of Arthur (centre) and Guinevere.

Heurodis. The theme of the wild hunt hinted at by the horn, dog and hawk underscore this subtext of *Lanval*.

The perfect world of the lovers, in which amity reigns, provides a stark contrast to the imperfect world of Arthur's court, which – noble and great though it sometimes seems – is tawdry and petty in comparison. The farcical justice of the judicial court called by Arthur to try Lanval simply provides an emphatic microcosm of the failings of the larger context of the king's retinue. The queen's false accusations of homosexuality and failed seduction provide a telling contrast to Lanval's joy with his true love, with which figure – herself an echo of the ancient Sovranty goddess – the knight has consummated a very real and far more meaningful relationship. Indeed, Lanval's love's association with Lady Sovranty is all the more pronounced through her stark contrast with the worldly Queen Guinevere, whose pettiness belies the nobility of the court of Arthur: whereas the ancient myths suggest that the consort of Lady Sovranty is by definition fit to rule, Arthur's relationship with his queen illuminates and even exacerbates this pathetic king's base and craven nature, which so easily would exchange justice for domestic tranquillity.

Too good for the shallow and self-serving world of Arthur's court, Lanval seeks permanent refuge in the otherworld of his fairy lady, recapturing her affection and earning his entry into this alternate existence through his steadfast and almost superhuman love, a passion which abides even in the face of the abandonment and rejection wrought by his thoughtless betrayal of his vow to his lover.[23] The fact that the otherworld in question is explicitly identified as Avalon emphasizes the mythic and folkloric associations of the fairy realm in this text.[24] The fairy lady's return to save and reclaim her erstwhile lover is embroidered with majesty and pageantry, beauty and power. Reflecting from afar some of the fundamental attributes of the Sovranty figure of old, Lanval's lady offers him power, prestige and majesty otherwise entirely beyond the reach or even the ken of ordinary mortals; indeed, the comparatively base and beggarly court of Arthur recognizes the station of such a figure only through the ostentatious display of her wealth, while the subtler senses of her true love are engaged by her beauty and worthiness alone. Certainly, far more nobly than the ancient kings who earned the right to rule through their union with such a Sovranty figure, Lanval wishes for none of the pomp and circumstance – and yet all the affection and love – of his otherworldly lady.

The 'fairy lover' or 'fairy mistress' is a commonplace of British and Irish folklore that is manifested in a number of medieval Arthurian texts.[25] This concept is drawn from a rich vein of mythic material, and ultimately may be derived from the Old Irish term *lennan side*, meaning (more or less) 'fairy lover'.[26] Although this fairy lover is most often female, variations concerning a male fairy exist, in which the lover is extremely handsome in appearance and courtly in manner, but of a despotic and powerful character which bespeaks the tremendous and terrifying forces of nature represented by the fairies, powers which always reside just beneath the polished and placid surface they present to ordinary humans.

In the more common case of a female fairy lover, the basic story of her affair with her mortal consort generally follows a standard format. The mortal lover meets and falls desperately in love with the fairy lover, who consents to the affair under certain restraints or conditions. Later, the mortal somehow breaks the covenant, thereby apparently losing the fairy lover forever. The mortal seeks to regain the love of the fairy through a variety of efforts, and although these are often in vain, sometimes the lovers are reunited. In some cases the reunion is due to superlative efforts or suffering on the part of the mortal. In others, however, the mortal hardly seems particularly deserving, and sometimes – although far more rarely – a reconciliation is brought about by the fairy, who suffers the pangs of absent love. The fairy lover motif also is sometimes rendered as a form of dominatrix who yearns for broad powers of control over the affections and affairs of men in general. In the case of *Lanval*, however, the fairy lover is presented as a paragon of virtue and justice as well as of beauty, and thus both Arthur and his queen act as foils whose flaws emphasize the terrible imperfections of even the very best this world has to offer.

## The folkloric English face of an Arthurian hero

### *Sir Gawain and the Green Knight* and the mythic trope of the beheading contest

Preserved in a single tome, Cotton Nero A.x., dated to circa 1375, *Sir Gawain and the Green Knight* seems to have been the work of the same author who composed *Pearl*, *Purity* and *Patience*, three additional and very different poems also found in this one manuscript source. The most important of the other poems is generally agreed to be *Pearl*, and for this reason the sole compilation volume containing these poems is generally referred to as the 'Gawain Manuscript' or the 'Pearl Manuscript', and its author is usually known as the 'Gawain Poet' or the 'Pearl Poet'. Written in a dialect of the northwest Midlands, which is challenging in terms of both orthography and lexicon, *Sir Gawain*, unlike the roughly contemporaneous works of Chaucer, is best known to most modern readers through translation, a fact which renders somewhat opaque to general readers its rich use of alliterative verse, its distinct 'bob and wheel' rhyme scheme at the end of each stanza and its subsequent place of pride in the 'Alliterative Revival' of the fourteenth century.

The vibrant imagery of the poem, however, shines through even the most workmanlike translations, and some aspects of the fabulous mythic and folkloric traditions which gave birth to the central episodes of this narrative may be discerned with even the most cursory effort. The poem is divided into four sections, called 'fitts', which concern, respectively, the arrival of the Green Knight in the court of King Arthur at Christmastide and the ensuing 'beheading game' bargain; Sir Gawain's journey in search of the Green Chapel and his arrival at a mysterious castle at which much of the central action of the poem takes place; a three-day series of hunts in the field and related temptation sequences in Gawain's bedchamber; and the final denouement at the Green Chapel, in which Gawain is repaid in kind for the blow he gave to the Green Knight in the initial episode.[27]

If the ancient lore at the heart of this poem teaches us anything at all, it may be: 'be careful what you wish for.' Arthur's headstrong foolishness in this regard sets the entire action of *Sir Gawain* into motion: the wild young king tempts fate by declaring that he will not partake of the holiday feast until he has seen or heard of some marvellous wonder or feat of arms. Like Pwyll, Head of Annwvn, in the First Branch of the Welsh *Mabinogion* – who sought to see a wonder from the top of Gorsedd Arberth, even though warned that he would either see a marvel or feel a blow for his trouble – Arthur gets much more than he had bargained for, in his case through the agency of a marvel of a visitor who offers a wondrous contest.

The marvellous wonder which appears bearing this incredible challenge is none other than the Green Knight himself, who, in addition to his eponymous hue, is clad in verdant raiment instead of armour, embroidered all over with natural imagery including the forms of birds and butterflies. As if the colour of this otherworldly visitor should not be enough to offer a clue as to his links to the natural world and its elemental powers, his clothing, his horse and its gear, as well as the holly bob he bears in his hand, all serve to underscore the visitor's identity as the 'Green Man', his function as a fertility figure and his powers over burgeoning life and sudden death, the dichotomy of which is emphasized by the fact that the Green Knight bears holly in one hand and his great axe in the other.

The axe both symbolizes the Green Knight's power to deal out deathly blows and serves as the agent through which such carnage may be dispensed. Moreover, the holly bob he carries in his opposite hand signifies the life that may spring forth and flourish even in the depths of winter, the earth's seasonal death: the holly plant, which exudes the promise of life in the midst of death, blossoms in bright colourful green and red in the dull setting of the forest in winter, when other signs of vibrancy lie dormant. The dark green leaves of the holly symbolize the same forces of vitality which the Green Knight himself represents, while the crimson berries evoke the life force of the blood coursing through the Green Man's veins, a potent power released through ritual sacrifice in order to ensure that in spring new life will burgeon in the seemingly sterile fields of winter.

It is of particular significance that – as Gawain points out – it is beneath the dignity of Arthur to partake in the 'Christmas game' proposed by the Green Knight; this assertion resonates with the exception of the chieftains Conchobar and Fergus from the beheading game offered by a monstrous challenger at the court of Emain Macha in the *Fled Bricrenn*.[28] It is also noteworthy that this theme of the game seems self-consciously couched in a repetitive language of games and play throughout the story of Gawain's encounter with the Green Knight. Unlike the Orthodox traditions of the East, which emphasized the sanctity of Easter, in Northern Europe Christmas was the greatest holiday of the year, and as such was marked by a long schedule of festive activities, including games, disguises and gift-giving.

Indeed, in the medieval England that produced *Sir Gawain and the Green Knight,* the Christmas season marked a wide-ranging festival bracketed by the Nativity on 25 December and the Epiphany on 6 January. These 'Twelve Days of Christmas' combined a long holiday from labour with a number of disparate traditions. New Year's Day falls right in the middle of this period, and was associated with gift-giving, a fact which the *Gawain* poet weaves into the fabric of the story. Other traditions included ancient British folk rituals concerning holly and other evergreen plants representing the rebirth of life in the midst of death, as well as heavily pagan-influenced Christian celebrations of the reassertion of light in the season of darkness once celebrated by pre-Christian Romans in the festival of Saturnalia. There were also some Scandinavian equivalents, including the celebration of *Jol*, or 'Yule', a term which has come to be associated with the Feast of the Nativity in English, but which originally designated a pagan fire ceremony or ritual purification and rebirth at midwinter.

Notably, 'Christmas games' in the fourteenth century included the exchange of 'handsels', or New Year's gifts, and the practice of mumming, especially as this practice was manifested in the form of the 'Wild Man of the Woods' theme and impressive 'special effects', which might even include pyrotechnics. Elaborate masks and costumes – as well as related short dramatic interludes – were immensely popular at the time, and some later developed into large-scale plays. However, mumming also provided an anonymous opportunity to cast aside inhibitions and protocol, as well as offering an ideal context for criminal activity, and in large urban areas such as London such disguises and related boisterous behaviour was often outlawed.

In such a context of mumming, the Green Knight's decapitation at the start of the poem takes on the trappings of an elaborate and gruesome performance, which might explain why the shock of the audience gives way so quickly to a blasé return to the feast, complete with 'double portions'. Further, given the tradition of handsels, Gawain's 'gift exchange' contest with his host may be seen in a more prosaic light, as may his acquisition of the green girdle. That said, the symbolism of fertility and Christmas customs of gift-giving and elaborate costuming are hardly mutually exclusive, and it is even tempting to underscore yet again that the Christmas season in medieval Britain was rife with ancient pagan practices dressed up as Christian celebrations.

The theme of the 'Green Man' and its relationship to the Green Knight in this poem has been the subject of some debate. Although some scholars have seen in the Green Knight an obvious manifestation of an ancient fertility figure, others have noted the lack of evidence for such a figure in Celtic mythology, as well as the fact that the folkloric evidence for something approaching a cult of the Green Man – a May Day figure perhaps linked to fertility festivals and licentiousness – can be traced back with reasonable reliability only a few centuries. In addition, although many stone carvings certainly attest to the popularity of what has been dubbed the 'foliate head', a decorative tradition which depicts human features within a context of burgeoning vegetative growth, there is no direct evidence explicitly linking such sculpture with contemporary or ancient fertility rites. It is also unclear that any literary tradition of the Green Man is related to this artistic motif. Having acknowledged these facts, it is only fair to note the fertility themes developed by the poet which clearly seem to link the decapitation episodes in *Sir Gawain and the Green Knight*.

Descriptions of the visiting knight mention his signature colour a number of times. Moreover, it is not his vibrant colour alone in which we may perceive a possible relationship between this verdant giant, the natural world and the changing seasons with which he may be linked: his garments and gear are well-embroidered, we are told, with intricate designs too numerous to recount. Thus, although the poet mentions little other detail, he makes a point of noting that birds and butterflies (classic symbols of the burgeoning life force which, although slumbering at the midwinter of the knight's appearance, promises to burst forth in spring and summer) make up part of the design.

Furthermore, the knight himself is described in a language of the natural world – we are told, for example, that his great beard resembles a mighty green bush. Moreover, we are informed that the court are dumbstruck by the fact that – like unto the grass, as the poet puts it – a chevalier and his cheval should have sprouted and flourished so green. Perhaps most notable of all are the twin symbols of life and death in the grim grip of the Green Knight: in one hand he holds a holly bob which – our informant is quick to point out – is at its most vitally verdant when the rest of the forest lies grey and fallow; in the other hand, meanwhile, the visitor grasps the handle of an axe, the sharp killing edge of which is mounted on a well-turned handle of wood wound about with iron embossed all in green, with a thong twisted around it decorated with tassels and pendants of a vibrant green hue. The life and death sitting side by side in these twin symbols is clearly manifested when Gawain takes the axe to the head of the Green Knight, releasing a flood of crimson – the colour of the holly berries – upon the great green field of his breast. The relationship between the person of the Green Knight and the natural world which he represents is thus underscored, just as the ancient and widespread practice of the sacrifice of a 'Corn King' to ensure the rebirth of the dormant winter fields in the coming spring might be said to be evoked.

Indeed, should the symbolic relationship between the Green Knight and the natural world of seed, stem and leaf be lost upon the casual reader, the poet's description of the change of seasons at the start of the second fitt helps to reinforce this resonance; moreover, given the winter setting of the tremendous bulk of the poem, the brief description of the rest of the year stands out in sharp relief. The entire narrative is clearly framed by the dual episodes of the exchange of blows, episodes which both take place in the depths of midwinter, right around the time of the solstice.

It is this timing, in part, which has led some scholars to posit that the Green Knight is some sort of literary echo – however distant and faint – of the figure of the sacrificial Corn King. Common throughout the world, the Corn King is a leader, hero – or sometimes

The engraving shows a child floating on a small boat, asleep.
At its feet rest a spear, a shield and a helmet.

god – who sacrifices himself to provide plenty for his people. Such sacrifices, it has been suggested, might very well take place during the coldest and darkest time of the year, when – especially in the northern latitudes – the long, cold, dark night of the midwinter solstice might be thought to demand such a sacrifice to ensure the renewal of the Sun, the rebirth of the seemingly moribund seeds within the grave of the earth and thus the survival of mankind. Many have noted, for example, that it is hardly a coincidence that Christ and Mithras are celebrated at festivals at this time.

Moreover, some medieval literary evidence – in addition to later verifiable folk beliefs and practices – concerning various beneficial 'corn spirits' and even fearsome 'corn demons' is highly suggestive in the context of the *Gawain* poet's description of the Green Knight. William of Malmesbury attested in the early twelfth century to an Anglo-Saxon belief in a foundling named Sceaf, that is to say 'Sheaf', a young boy with a pillow made of a sheaf of grain who was discovered in the vicinity of Scandia adrift in a boat with no oars. Numerous scholars have suggested that this episode comprises an ancient myth explaining the arrival of agriculture in 'Scandinavia'. If this thesis is correct, it may well illuminate the opening sequence of the great Anglo-Saxon epic *Beowulf*, in which Scyld Scefing, 'Shield, son of Sheaf', the progenitor of the Danish royal house, was set adrift in a great, treasure-laden funeral ship which took the body of the dead king to an unknown destination; the poet notes that this was an especially appropriate departure for a ruler who had arrived as an orphaned child, all alone on a drifting barge. In any case, it is certain that a figure called Sceaf is mentioned in a number of royal Anglo-Saxon genealogies.

An even more pertinent and explicit example of otherworldly 'corn spirits', however, was recorded in the late twelfth century by William of Newburgh, a notably hard-headed critic of Geoffrey of Monmouth who might be expected to vet his sources with some care and even cynicism. Nevertheless, according to this account, farmers during the reign of King Stephen in the middle years of the twelfth century came upon a strange boy and girl in the midst of fields being harvested by reapers. The children were entirely green, wore otherworldly clothing and – once they had been taught the tongue of the land in which they found themselves – claimed to have come from what sounded like a fairy realm on the far banks of a broad river. These children were so clearly identified with the crops in the field, moreover, that they had to be taught to consume bread, as their instinct was to survive upon freshly shucked beans. The green pigment alone seems enough to suggest that these children are manifestations of corn spirits, although the identification with the fields and preference for fresh beans helps to flesh out this association. In any case, this episode serves to emphasize the fact that it is not a tremendous stretch to suggest that the Green Knight who faces Gawain may well likewise be perceived as a figure associated with fertile fields and harvest rituals.[29]

The cycle of the year is a crucial element of a harvest ritual, and thus it is noteworthy that the Gawain poet emphasizes the centrality of midwinter to this narrative by describing the passing of time in terms which underscore the greening and subsequent greying of the fields and forests. Indeed, the entire intervening year between the otherworldly visitor's appearance at the court of King Arthur and the date of Sir Gawain's pledged departure to seek the Green Chapel is shoe-horned into two stanzas. Although such compression of time – like the formulaic description of the trials and ordeals of the quest that follows – is a typical narrative component of the medieval romance, the poet's emphasis on the turning of the seasons is worthy of some examination: the emphasis of these stanzas is on the life cycle of the natural world as this is made manifest through the passage from vegetative dormancy into burgeoning growth, followed by abundance which is replaced by decay and rot and the semblance of death until the cycle begins anew.

The green girdle offered by the lady of the castle to Sir Gawain as a protective talisman itself manifests an overt fertility theme, as well as evoking a folkloric motif concerning the weaving, spinning and wearing of textiles of this nature – an activity which spanned thousands of years in Europe seems to have been prevalent throughout the Middle Ages and continues in more easterly regions even up to the present day. Although the poet's description of the girdle in question only mentions that it was comprised of bright green silk adorned with gold and ornately embroidered around the edges, these signature colours themselves seem of obvious significance in this context, resonating as they do with both the burgeoning fertility of the growing fields of spring and the burnished grain of an abundant harvest.

The fact that the girdle was taken from the presumably fertile and certainly sexually attractive hips of the lady is also a point worthy of note, most especially in the context of the multifaceted powers of womanly magic represented by the wife and her companion the crone, who is herself later identified as Morgan le Fay, a figure widely identified with potent magic. Here she is a sorceress of considerable power, as evidenced by her ability to transform Lord Bertilak into the Green Knight and to allow him to survive an apparent decapitation at the hands of Gawain. The host himself later names her a 'goddess' of immense powers, and notes her own sexual prowess and powers in her dealings with Merlin, of which, Lord Bertilak seems confident, every Knight of the Round Table was well informed.

This context of sexuality seems particularly fitting given the theme of agricultural fertility associated with the figure of the Green Knight. Thus the lady's sexual temptations of Gawain are more than mere plot devices, and Gawain's desire to protect his head by girding his loins using a symbolically charged textile with associations with agricultural abundance seems to suggest that life-giving forces may be evoked to deter those of life-taking. It is also noteworthy that belief in such enchanted belts and girdles was widespread in medieval England, and extended to particular patterns associated with feminine fecundity, physical protection and even safety in childbirth.[30]

The 'beheading game' motif is represented in a number of medieval romances – of which *Sir Gawain* is but the most famous – and is present in a number of heroic works as well. Such a game is most notably employed, in fact, in the Irish *Fled Bricrenn*, in which a giant bachlach offers to engage in a similar contest at the court of Emain Macha, although – unlike the Green Knight – the bachlach insists that he should deal the first blow.[31] Although hardly proof of ancient rites of human sacrifice in and of themselves, these multiple literary examples certainly suggest an intriguing medieval literary fascination with decapitation that is at the least worthy of close examination. This is not to claim that the roots of these traditions are discernible ancient practices of human sacrifice, but rather to point out that it is possible – if difficult to prove – that they could be.[32] Moreover, it is certain that decapitation is a common theme in early Welsh and Irish literature and mythology, and there is some classical evidence that head-hunting was an important practice of the early Celts. Actual or symbolic sacrifice at midwinter to guarantee the rebirth of the Sun and the growing year was a commonplace of the ancient world, reflected in myths of figures including such notables as Mithras and Jesus, to name but two of the better known. In any case, *Sir Gawain* is replete with mythic and folkloric material, and the beheading sequences are particularly rich veins in this regard. In short, when he enters the court of King Arthur, the Green Knight brings into the Arthurian canon a host of elements with which to inform our study.

The tales we have examined in this chapter all present Arthurian themes, storylines and characters that reverberate with the echoes of ancient myths, legends and folklore. In the discussion of archetypal Arthurian objects which follows, we will likewise hear suggestive snatches of ancient myths and folklore which will inform our investigations of the common understandings of some of the most well-known and well-loved aspects of medieval British literature.

ra ete pas ſer oue-Dnr 18 eu
gnidoir le main qui iſſoir hors du
lac qui priſt leſpee le roy artu·

⸿uant gyrfles voit que
faire li conuient· sire
uient arriere la ou leſ
pee eſtoit ſi la prent ⁊ la recomē
ce a regarder ⁊ a plaindre mlt
durement ⁊ dist tot en plorant·
ha? eſpee borne ⁊ bele plus que nu
le autre rant eſt grās damages
de vos· quant ƥ ne chaes es mais
de ƥzeudome· lors la lance el lac

Miniature of Girflet watching as Arthur's sword
is retrieved by a hand emerging from the lake.

# 2

# Legendary Treasures
of Avalon

E voking an aura as potent as that of the figure of King Arthur himself are some of the most famous objects associated with him. The most well-known of these are emblematic of Avalon and of all things Arthur. The terms 'Excalibur', the 'Round Table' and the 'Holy Grail' have, over the centuries, taken on an almost totemic power.

## Excalibur: the sword of Arthur

Aside from the Holy Grail itself, Excalibur is arguably the single most recognizable object in the Arthurian canon, and this sword's potent mythic, legendary and folkloric resonance have imbued the name with an enduring power. From a very early point in the Arthurian tradition, King Arthur's signature weapon neatly encapsulated the hero's epic dimensions and supernatural qualities and connections. For example, Geoffrey of Monmouth, Wace and Layamon all agree that this magical blade was forged in Avalon, thus emphasizing the otherworldly nature and powers it represented. Robert Mannyng of Brunne claimed that this mighty blade spanned 10 full feet (3 metres), and that it remained an heirloom of the British Crown, being given as a peace offering in 1191 from Richard i to his former enemy Tancred of Sicily. Further evidence of the sword's magical properties and mythical provenance were the prophesies that Arthur would not lose in any battle in which he carried Excalibur and that he would avoid grievous wounds and loss of blood so long as he kept its scabbard by his side.[1]

The Herefordshire priest known to posterity as Layamon, who completed *Brut* in the decade before 1200, paid special attention to

Arthur's arms and armour, objects which are often thought to have mythical and magical qualities. He follows both Geoffrey and Wace, for instance, in attributing to Arthur the powerful blade *Caliburnus*, a Latin form of the Welsh name *Caledfwlch*, which is itself seemingly cognate with the Irish *Caladbolg*; in Old French this name was rendered *Escalibor*, which eventually comes down to us through Malory as 'Excalibur'. The ultimate source for this name may have been an ancient Celtic word meaning something like 'hard striker'.[2] The *Historia regum Britanniae*, *Roman de Brut* and *Brut* all concur that this weapon came from Avalon and was powerfully enchanted. Layamon agrees with Geoffrey that Arthur's shield was called Pridwen, the name given in *Culhwch and Olwen* and elsewhere for Arthur's ship; however that may be, this shield, so the *Historia* and *Brut* both inform us, was adorned within with an image of the Virgin Mary, just as was Gawain's in his journey to seek the Green Knight. Layamon further describes Arthur's helmet and mail in some detail: Goswhit, 'Goosewhite', the former, was an heirloom from Uther, wrought of steel and encrusted with gems set in gold; Wygar, the latter, was forged, we are told, of steel rings at the hand of an elfin smith identified as Witege, variously read as a 'wise one' – a wizard – or as 'Widia', the son of Weland, the Great smith of Anglo-Saxon mythology.

According to the most famous version of the story composed by Malory, Arthur received Excalibur from the Lady of the Lake, and thus it is not to be confused with the sword drawn from the stone, which, according to *Le Morte Darthur*, Arthur shattered in combat with Pellinore; indeed, it was as a result of this very mishap that Merlin cast a spell of sleep upon Arthur's opponent so that he might lead the king to the Lady of the Lake and gain for him Excalibur. Malory himself, however, seems to have succumbed in one instance to the temptation of conflating these two blades: early in *Le Morte Darthur*, when the young Arthur was still attempting to quell the rebellious lesser kings and consolidate his kingdom, he is said to have drawn Excalibur, which blinded his enemies with the brightness of thirty torches. Supernatural glow aside, the order of events makes it clear that this could not be the sword gifted to Arthur by the Lady of the Lake, a weapon that he had not, at the point of that particular battle, yet received.

Miniature of King Arthur, holding a spear and
a shield emblazoned with the Virgin and Child.

At the end of Arthur's earthly life and reign this magical sword
was to be returned to its watery home, a task delegated to Bedivere
in *Le Morte Darthur*, although others perform it in alternate versions.
According to Malory, Bedivere twice pretended to have cast the
wondrous blade away, only to be chastised by the dying Arthur, who
did not believe the sword had been returned to its proper home until
Bedivere correctly described the vision of the hand that had sprung
from the deeps to catch Excalibur in mid-flight and shake it three
times before drawing it down into the lake. Some have suggested
that this ceremonial return of Arthur's sword into the depths is evocative of the ancient practice – common in Northern Europe, and
clearly attested in both the literary and archaeological records – of
making votive offerings to the gods in pools and swamps; others see
it as an echo of an ancient funeral sacrifice, wherein the dead man's
most valuable and potent treasures and weapons were dedicated to
the deceased so that they might accompany him on his journey to
the otherworld.

Excalibur as the name for Arthur's sword was popularized by *Le Morte Darthur*. Although many modern scholars think that this name is related to the Welsh term *caled*, meaning 'hard',[3] Malory himself followed his source's etymology of the name, which was 'steel cutter', said by some to be derived from the Latin *chalybs*, a term for 'steel' used substantively in some contexts to suggest 'sword'.[4] This name appeared in Old French as *Escalibor* and in Latin as *Caliburnus*, the label Geoffrey of Monmouth attributes to the blade Arthur carried against the Saxons at Bath and the Romans under Lucius, as well as before the gates of Paris in single combat against the Roman governor Frollo. Arthur's weapon is referred to in a number of Welsh sources as *Caledfwlch*, perhaps most notably in *Culhwch and Olwen*, wherein it was one of Arthur's great treasures that he reserved from his young kinsman when he offered to fulfil nearly any boon Culhwch might ask. Caledfwlch was also the weapon used by Llenlleawg Wyddel to slay the Irish giant Diwrnach Wyddel, keeper of a Cauldron of Plenty which also makes an appearance in the Second Branch of the *Mabinogion*. Many scholars also suggest a link between this Welsh ancestor of Excalibur and its Irish counterpart *Caladbolg*, 'Hard Lightning Bolt' or 'Heavy Missile', the lightning blade of Fergus mac Róich, as well as with the Breton *Kaledvoulch*.[5] In any case, it seems likely from this arsenal of ancient Irish and Welsh weaponry that Excalibur has a long and distinguished mythic lineage, and that the signature weapon of the medieval King Arthur was forged in the smithies of Celtic gods and heroes lost in the mist of time.

## The Round Table: a gathering of heroes

If Excalibur is the object most closely associated with King Arthur in the modern imagination, the Round Table is the emblem which represents Arthur's court and his collection of heroes, who are collectively remembered in the popular consciousness as the 'Knights of the Round Table'. According to much lore, Arthur attracted the best of the best. In fact, as early as the *Historia regum Britanniae*, Geoffrey of Monmouth asserted the primacy of the court of Arthur across Europe, reporting that the fame of Arthur and his court was such that aristocrats throughout all of Europe dressed and acted in the manner of Arthur's knights, and therefore it should come as no surprise that the finest knights were drawn to Arthur. Thus Geoffrey provides us with a seed from which the concept of the Knights of the Round Table might be thought to have taken root, to blossom later in such works as that of Malory.

Although heavily indebted to Geoffrey's *Historia* for many of its major plot points, Wace's *Roman de Brut* contains a number of significant alterations from its source material. Most vital among the innovations introduced by Wace may be the concept of the Round Table, the iconic gathering place of Arthur's knights at which each has equal standing.[6] Wace claims a Breton source for the notion of the Round Table, which as a specific object is not mentioned in the

The wooden Round Table has been hanging in the Grand Hall, Winchester, since 1348, with the names of 24 knights inscribed on it in letters of gold. It was painted in 1522 at the orders of Henry VIII.

*Historia*, although Geoffrey clearly describes the general nature of Arthur's court in somewhat similar terms. Wace extends the earlier theme of Arthur's court as the maker of fashions, the destination for all who might aspire to join the ranks of the most elite warriors of the aristocracy of all of Europe, describing the Round Table as just such a gathering place for any knight who might wish to be thought courteous and worldly, or who might seek to gain in wealth as well as glory. In fact, any knight who appeared without the clothing, customs and courtesy current in Arthur's court, Wace tells us, would seem uncivilized and boorish.

Introduced by Wace and subsequently developed more fully by Layamon, the concept of the Round Table included the belief that its shape would help defuse arguments over precedence, as each man would be seated at an equal distance from the centre.[7] Although it may seem obvious, traditional rectangular tables necessarily place some seats much further than others from the head of the table, a fact which informs rules of precedence and protocol to this day. Since medieval etiquette dictated that those seated nearest to their lord were of a higher rank than and took precedence over those seated farther away, this creation seems to have been designed specifically to avoid any such dissension: no man seated at it might claim a higher station than his neighbour, and all who were members of that select company were as brothers; none was treated as an outcast or a foreigner. Some sources, like Béroul's twelfth-century *Tristan*, actually propose that the table rotates, a concept perhaps most fully realized in the fourteenth-century Icelandic adaptation *Skikkju rimur*, in which Arthur sits in the midst of his knights upon a circular throne which turns like the Sun, so that each retainer may bask in Arthur's brilliance for an equal period.[8]

Although the number of those seated around the Round Table is not mentioned by Wace, later traditions range widely, although thirteen is a significant number, evoking as it does the disciples gathered with Christ for the Last Supper. In any case the Round Table is, even in its earliest version, an important mythic addition to the Arthurian tradition, offering as it does both a specific place and a particular way in which Arthur gathers with his followers. As this concept evolved and its resonance with the Last Supper and the subsequent Grail tradition became more clearly developed, the Round

Table – like the Grail itself – became a trope which links King Arthur more and more powerfully to the mythic archetype of the dying god.

Layamon also develops the existing notion of the Round Table in two major ways. The first concept concerning the Round Table introduced in the English *Brut* is a more detailed description of the background events leading to the construction of this object: Layamon reports that a massive brawl erupted in Arthur's court over the question of precedence. It happened one Christmas that representatives and retainers gathered in London from all the far-flung corners of Arthur's dominion, all seated and served in order of rank. It soon came to pass, however, that many were displeased with their assigned stations and a violent riot erupted that was only stemmed when Arthur quelled it with the aid of a hundred fully armed and armoured men. To ensure that the king's peace might never be broken again, Arthur made an example of the instigator of the brawl, annihilating his clan in order to make the royal point: in an execution strikingly reminiscent of the bog sacrifices of old, Arthur had the malefactor dragged from the court by a noose around the neck and drowned in a bog; the male members of that entire family were beheaded, while the females had their noses cropped off to mar their beauty and thus to ensure that no man would desire them.

Layamon's second innovation regarding the Round Table is a magical element concerning the construction of this masterpiece of carpentry. The debacle of the Christmas brawl ultimately led a talented Cornish artisan to offer to construct for the king a Round Table to dispense with such foolish concerns of precedence forever-more. This table, we are told, could seat more than 1,600, and because of its shape each man would sit in equity, offering only toasts to his brothers alongside him. The skill of the maker was such, *Brut* informs us, that his creation, capacious as it was, might be collapsed and trans-ported easily alongside the king as he rode, in order to move with Arthur's court and be suitable for any venue of the king's choosing, despite its enormous size when it was deployed.

Some medieval artists depicted the Round Table as a ring, and if one envisions Arthur's seat as situated in the centre of such a ring, one might grasp the idea of equidistance associated with the Round Table, a concept which echoes a tradition ascribed to ancient Celtic war bands: according to this belief, Celtic warriors of old surrounded their chieftain, sitting in a circle around him.[9] Wace's claim of a Breton source for the notion of the Round Table might thus offer some slight support for the theory that this model in fact may have derived from just such an ancient Celtic practice. The idea of the Round Table suggested by Wace had been refined still further by the time of Malory, comprising at one and the same time an heirloom of the Pendragon dynasty, a bridal gift, a link to the Holy Grail and an emblem of the unity of the chivalric world.

Both the *Merlin* of Robert de Boron and the account of the Vulgate Cycle attribute the construction of the Round Table to Uther Pendragon, who was, so the story goes, acting under the instructions of Merlin. Uther subsequently gave the table to the father of Guinevere, who returned this gift to the House of Pendragon upon the occasion of his daughter's marriage to Arthur. Later authors, notably Malory, extensively refine the concept of the Round Table, finding precedents in those tables associated with the Last Supper and the Holy Grail. The Round Table – according to these sources, which Malory follows fairly closely – was meant to symbolize the table at which Christ met with his disciples for the Last Supper; furthermore, the Round Table evoked the tradition of the Grail Table, a concept echoed in the *Chronicle* of John Hardyng. The Grail Table was itself a reflection of the table of Christ, which thus serves as the prototype, not simply for the physical furniture involved, but for both the sacred mystic conclave of the Grail and the secular chivalric community of the Round Table. The Grail Table, we are told, was founded by Joseph of Arimathea at the behest of the Holy Ghost.

According to the Vulgate Cycle account, the shape of the table was meant to signify the whole chivalric world, in that knights from around that world were joined in its brotherhood; Malory, on the other hand, seems to indicate the more prosaic idea that the shape was meant to reflect the physical shape of the world. The purported number of seats at the Round Table varied according to the account, and the tally ranged widely; indeed, even Malory contradicted himself at different points, citing both 140 and 150 as the correct figure. The number thirteen is often cited, as we have seen, thus making explicit the link between the Knights of the Round Table and the Disciples

at the Last Supper, an analogy which renders manifest Arthur's identification with Christ, and thus with the archetype of the dying god.

## The Siege Perilous: the hot seat at the round table

A number of traditions developed over time concerning the magical
properties of the Round Table relative to the knights joined in its
community; for example, some sources – notably the early thirteenth-
century *Daniel* of Der Stricker – claim that the table itself might reject
any prospective member not morally fit to be seated in that community. This concept is very closely related to the theme of the Siege
Perilous, the 'dangerous seat', in which only the chosen knight might
sit. Just as some sources cite thirteen as the number of seats at the
Round Table, analogous to those at the Last Supper, there are those
– such as Boron's *Merlin* – which identify the Siege Perilous with the
seat vacated by Judas at that meal. A similar seat at the Grail Table,
we are told by some sources, would actually destroy any unworthy
fool with the temerity to sit upon it.[10]

As we have seen, in some sources the Round Table was thought
to have been modelled after the Grail Table, which in turn was

Illustration of Sir Galahad taking his place at the Siege Perilous, from
the 15th-century *Quest for the Holy Grail* by Évrard d'Espinques.

modelled after the Table of Christ; in the same way, in the Vulgate Cycle the Siege Perilous was said to be a form of the seat of Josephus, which was in turn a form of the seat of Jesus.[11] This seat was left vacant, then, in anticipation of the arrival of the Grail Knight. Moreover, the title of the Siege Perilous, according to this schema, was earned through analogy with the seat of Josephus, in which one of two brothers earned utter destruction because, out of envy, he wished to displace Josephus.

In Gerbert de Montreuil's continuation to *Perceval*, the Siege Perilous is portrayed as a locus of judgement and an agent of justice – similar to Der Stricker's vision of the Round Table itself – upon the unrighteous who occupy it. According to this version of the tale, the Siege Perilous was an enchanted gift from the fairy world which sent six knights into the gaping maw of the earth for a foretaste of the tortures of hell until they were redeemed by Perceval himself; a rather homophobic epilogue to this tale implies that these knights were condemned for their preference of men rather than women. In another text which emphasizes the destructive qualities of the Siege Perilous, *Lancelot*, Sir Brumand is immolated for occupying that seat in a rash attempt to outdo Lancelot himself. The common assumption is that the only knight who would be able to sit upon the Siege Perilous without fear would be he who was destined to complete the Grail quest successfully; in Malory this knight is, of course, Galahad, whose name marvellously appears upon the dreadful chair.[12]

## The Holy Grail: the object of the great quest of Avalon

The Holy Grail, as it appears in Malory's work, is the result of centuries of medieval working and reworking of themes from a number of quite distinct founts. Whichever source a reader favours, it is probably fair to say that – whatever came first or whichever might have influenced another – the Grail as Malory depicts it resonates with several distinct sets of sympathetic mythic structures. Thus ancient Near Eastern ritual practices, Celtic folkloric fertility motifs and Christian symbolism are fused by the time of *Le Morte Darthur* into an archetypal object which intertwines themes of sacred healing, sustenance and plenty, and the hope of spiritual salvation.[13]

The term 'grail' comes from the French word *graal*, meaning 'platter', which is itself derived from the Latin *gradale*, meaning any 'dish' upon which a given course, or *gradus*, of a meal might be served. The name originally carried no specific valence, then, and in some early sources the object to which the term refers, although certainly noteworthy and magical, has not yet become the most sacred object of Christian veneration and sanctified quest that the Holy Grail is taken to be in Malory.[14] Indeed, Chrétien de Troyes indicates through his use of the indefinite article – *un graal*, or 'a platter' – that the vessel of which he speaks, though marvellous and imbued with fantastic powers, is not *the* one true and unique 'Holy' Grail of later Arthurian works.[15]

One of the most popular schools of thought concerning the Grail's origin suggests that the development of the Fisher King figure draws upon the ancient influence of death and rebirth rituals derived from the eastern Mediterranean; these cults ultimately evoked the regeneration of the year and the agricultural bounty associated with the cycle of the seasons. The Fisher King, then, represents a form of the dying god, whose death and rebirth through a proscribed ritual will guarantee the fertility of his fallow and seemingly sterile land. Such a reading, it might be noted in passing, seems associated with sexual potency, as do the ritual objects of the spear and the chalice.

The second main theory regarding the genesis of the Grail suggests that the Grail story includes a number of elements from Celtic mythology, most notably the theme of the Cauldron of Plenty. This concept is well-attested in Welsh and Irish sources, and involves a vessel which provides endless sustenance in the manner of a cornucopia. This motif resonates with the tradition, present in the French Vulgate *Queste del Saint Graal* and most memorably enshrined in English literature in *Le Morte Darthur*, that the Grail provides each who beholds it with the food and drink which best pleases the beholder. The object of the quest described in Wolfram von Eschenbach's early thirteenth-century *Parzival* is a magic stone rather than a cup. *Parzival*'s Grail combines a sustenance theme like that of the cornucopia with a healing motif like that associated with the Near Eastern cult rituals, because Wolfram's Grail both magically provides food and miraculously preserves life.[16]

King Arthur's knights, gathered at the Round Table to celebrate Pentecost,
witness a vision of the Holy Grail.

The literary tradition of the search for the Grail also may have a
Welsh antecedent – Arthur's journey to a mystic realm in his quest
for the Cauldron of Plenty is found in *Preiddiau Annwfn*, or the
'Spoils of Annfwn', the treasure of the otherworld. Three ships full of
Arthur's men seek the Cauldron of Plenty in this ninth-century Welsh
tale, in which they encounter seemingly eternally youthful denizens
of the fortress guarding the treasure; only seven members of the
unsuccessful venture eventually return from the otherworld.[17] The
life-giving force and magical location of this cauldron seem very
similar to those of the Grail described by Malory.

It is also notable that the theme of the Cauldron of Plenty is
sometimes subject to significant inversions, such as the Cauldron
of Regeneration described in the Second Branch of the Welsh
*Mabinogion*, in which dead warriors cast into a magic cauldron
spring back to life, albeit without the power of speech. Such an

object transforms the theme of the life-giving force of the enchanted vessel, shifting the focus in some measure to the spiritual realm, emphasizing as it does not only the power to provide energy for the physical body, but the capacity to reanimate that body, seemingly by re-inspiriting it.[18]

Along similar lines, Chrétien de Troyes' suggestion in his late twelfth-century tale of Perceval that life may be maintained by the daily consumption of a single Eucharistic wafer taken from the Grail marks a conflation of the Celtic Cauldron of Plenty theme – which emphasizes a magic vessel's capacity to provide endless food for the physical body – with what we might term a liturgical and redemptive understanding of the Grail, which is concerned with the sustenance provided for the soul.

In his verse Grail romance *Joseph d'Arimathea*, composed around 1200 and sometimes known as *Le Roman de l'estoire dou Graal*, Robert de Boron developed just such a liturgically driven concept of the Grail. Boron overtly described the subject of this quest as the Cup of Christ, that is, as the actual dish used by Jesus to celebrate the Last Supper with his disciples, and subsequently by Joseph of Arimathea to catch Christ's blood as he died upon the Cross. According to such a reading, of course, the Grail must be understood not simply as *a* sacred vessel, but rather as *the* unique prototype of the sacred vessels used in the Mass.[19]

This rather slight narrative emendation, which might well be thought to articulate explicitly a theme which theretofore had been implicit in the Grail tradition, in actuality comprises a rather significant theological shift. In the context of the sacred significance of the chalice utilized in the Mass, an object with which the Last Supper is ritually re-enacted at every religious service, the actual cup used by Christ himself at that very meal is imbued with a profound holiness and may be thought to represent almost limitless miraculous power. Indeed, given that the miracle inherent in the Mass is the actual – and not merely symbolic – presence of Christ's blood and flesh in the wine and bread of communion, the concept of the Holy Grail, the original vessel itself, raises the mythic ante, as it were, suggesting an object which may offer the opportunity for an even more rarefied and direct link with the divine.

The final step in the process of transformation, through which the Grail was transmuted, as it were, from a symbolic vessel drawn from a number of mythic sources and imbued with various magical attributes, into a direct conduit through which a devout and worthy Christian seeker may directly approach and interact with the Divine through the literal body of Jesus, is achieved in the Vulgate Cycle's *La Queste del Saint Graal*.[20] In this text Galahad, finally successful in his endeavour, achieves a vision of the Grail which includes the appearance of Christ emerging bodily from the chalice. This is the version which Malory uses as the basis for his own denouement of the Grail quest, an episode comprising a quite literal act of transubstantiation: when the officiant lifted the Eucharist in the act of consecrating it, the onlookers watched in awe as it was transformed into the likeness of a child with a burning bright appearance; then the host was returned to the Grail. Christ himself then emerged and greeted Galahad and his companions, passing among them with the Grail and offering them with his own hands the Communion wafer, which all found more delightful to the taste than anything they had ever experienced. Christ then commanded Galahad to leave the realm of Logris, which had lost through its evil ways the anointment he had granted it through the presence of the Grail; Galahad was to proceed to the City of Sarras with the Grail, which would never return to its former home.

## The guardian of the Grail:
### the Fisher King and the bleeding lance

The Fisher King is the title given to the Guardian of the Grail. It is important to note that this figure sometimes is conflated with that of the Wounded King, although often the two figures are distinct.[21] The Wounded King has been maimed by a spear thrust through the legs – sometimes suggested as a wound through the thighs, other times described more graphically as a wound to the groin or genitals – which leaves him lame and his kingdom sterile and bereft of its former fecundity.[22] While the wound is crippling, painful and will not heal, the life of the king is magically preserved so that he bleeds but does not die; the curse upon the land may only be lifted if the king's wound is healed, which may only occur if the Grail Knight asks a particular question, a mystical query concerning the Grail and related objects or the wounds of the king; only this question will break the spell. The link between the king's wound and his country's curse explicitly evokes mythic archetypes concerning sacral kingship and that of the dying god.

In the eponymous late twelfth-century work by Chrétien de Troyes, Perceval is the Grail Knight instead of Galahad, who fills this role in Malory's work. Chrétien describes Perceval's encounter with a fisherman who invites him to spend the night; later Perceval meets an unnamed Wounded King, who is in fact the fisherman of his earlier acquaintance. While in the hall of the Wounded King, Perceval witnesses a procession including the Grail, a platter and a bleeding lance. Although intrigued by this wondrous sight, Perceval doesn't ask the Wounded King about it, thus prolonging the poor man's suffering and concurrently the sterility of the Wasted Kingdom. Chrétien does not name the Fisher King, he does not explicitly identify the bleeding lance as the Spear of Longinus, nor is his work complete; indeed, Perceval finally completes the Grail quest in the third continuation of Chrétien's story, written some fifty years later by an author known to us only as Manessier, about whom almost nothing else is known.[23]

Although Chrétien de Troyes failed to flesh out the identity of the Fisher King, other writers filled this vacuum in a number of ways. Robert de Boron provides this figure with a lineage linking him with the Passion of Christ and the Last Supper, identifying the Fisher King as Bron, the brother-in-law to Joseph of Arimathea and the grandfather of Perceval, who, according to Boron, succeeds Bron in this position. Alternatively, the *Estoire del Saint Graal* (like the *Queste del Saint Graal*, one of the five romances of the Vulgate Cycle) suggests that Bron's twelfth son, Alain le Gros, was in fact appointed to the post of protector of the Grail by Josephus, son of Joseph of Arimathea; commanded to feed a multitude, in this version of the tale Alain le Gros caught a single fish which – in a clear evocation of the loaves and the fishes miracle – multiplied to fill the need. Alain and his successors were thus, according to this narrative strand, dubbed the Rich Fishermen. In some versions of the story Joseph of Arimathea himself was the Fisher King.[24] Following the Grail Knight tradition established by Chrétien de Troyes, Wolfram von Eschenbach's *Parzival* reasserts the primacy of the title character as the Grail Knight. In *Parzival* the Fisher King is named Anfortas, and the title character fails to ask about either the Grail procession or the cause of the king's torment, thus prolonging the suffering of the languishing king.

A Celtic analogue to the Fisher King, mystically wounded and lamed by a spear, may be found in the story of Bran the Blessed from the Second Branch of the *Mabinogion*. Bran is mortally wounded by a poisoned spear, but he survives in the form of a magically preserved living decapitated head which accompanies his companions, the handful of British survivors of an ill-fated expedition to Ireland, throughout their wanderings in exile. The episodes in question clearly share some elements, and some have even suggested that additional compelling evidence of resonance between them is illustrated by the fact that the Fisher King is known as 'Bron' in the Grail quest described by Robert de Boron.

According to tradition, Longinus was the name of the Roman legionnaire who pierced the side of Jesus with his lance; the blood from this wound, according to tradition, displayed miraculous powers from the very moment of its release, curing some unspecified impairment of vision. It is hardly surprising – given the rich fabric of the traditions concerning the Cup of Christ, and most especially in the context of the closely related evocation of the sanctity of Christ's blood which ultimately led to the doctrine of Transubstantiation – that the spear which drew forth blood and water from the body of the Saviour on the Cross would become an object of mystical veneration. Although the bleeding lance described in Chrétien's *Perceval* is not explicitly identified as the Spear of Longinus, the First Continuation of this tale, completed around the year 1200, makes the claim that the spear in the Grail procession was indeed that used to wound Christ upon the Cross.

The Vulgate Cycle adds the twist that it was this very same spear which maimed the Wounded King. Conversely, in some sources Longinus' spear has the capacity to heal as well as to wound, a power which stems from the common belief in the power of Christ's blood to cure blindness. Thus the blood that drips from the bleeding lance into the Holy Grail is that of Christ, a fact which implicitly draws an analogy between the Grail procession and the ceremony of the Mass, which reaches its spiritual climax in the enactment of the miracle of Transubstantiation, through which the wine of the ritual becomes the blood of God.[25] Not incidentally, the suggestion that the Maimed King was wounded by a thrust from this same spear, a concept stated as fact in the Vulgate Cycle, strengthens that figure's association with Christ, and thus with the mythic archetype of the dying god.

Detail of a miniature of the coronation of Arthur, from a late 15th-century manuscript from the southern Netherlands.

# 3

# Arthur Ascendant

Scholars and readers alike generally praise Sir Thomas Malory's *Le Morte Darthur* as the pinnacle of the medieval Arthurian tradition in English; this work certainly has remained the primary synthesis of earlier Arthuriana for authors who have followed Malory, and thus is the fundamental fount of all things Arthur up until the present day. Although Malory drank deeply at the well of Arthuriana as he found it, he also added to, deleted from and ultimately transformed that tradition, perhaps most notably in his treatment of Lancelot, who becomes in *Le Morte Darthur* a central unifying character, a hero who serves as a more flawed and therefore human foil to a semi-divine Arthur clearly destined for apotheosis from the momentous and magical conception which precedes his first appearance in the narrative.

Indeed, some have argued persuasively that Lancelot's very failings in the context of his desire to be perfect render him the tragic hero who appealed so deeply to the author and then to the audience, who may see in this figure's noble failings a reflection of a doomed and vain desire for perfection. From this vantage point, *Le Morte Darthur* includes twin heroic narratives: while Arthur's story may be organized under the rubrics of overarching archetypes of the hero, Lancelot's tale provides a counterpoint, detailing the meteoric rise and inexorable fall of a noble hero full of promise who meets his demise precisely because of his tragic and all-too-human flaws.

Malory's omnibus version of the tales of King Arthur was completed nearly at the end of the Middle Ages, circa 1470, by a 'knight prisoner' who remains shadowy, although he was quite probably the lord of Newbold Revel in Warwickshire. Malory finished his great work shortly before his death. In 1485 Caxton printed what was to become for a long time the standard edition of Malory until the so-called 'Winchester Manuscript' was found in the library of that name in 1934. While Caxton's edition had added chapter headings, divided the text, changed some language and created a structure of some 21 sections following the arc of the Arthurian narrative, the Winchester Manuscript seemed more organically structured around eight discrete themes, and thus could be seen as a collection of autonomous romances.[1] Although ink has continued to spill for most of a century over whether this discovery suggests that Malory intended to compose a single monolithic work, it is certain that we may draw from his collection of tales a compelling and related series of Arthurian narratives that serve to inform one another, and from the aggregate of which we may perceive a coherent narrative arc.

Malory provides a particularly helpful compendium of Arthurian mythology as – among many other narrative threads and mythic, legendary and folkloric details – his work allows one rather intuitively to trace discernible and coherent trajectories of the most seminal archetypal structures of this mythology. These include a miraculous conception, childhood deeds, adventures, battles, quests, death, a journey to the otherworld and apotheosis. The work also provides a particularly well-structured account of the mighty Grail quest, in addition to well-developed place and object myths concerning iconic features of the Arthurian tradition, including Excalibur, the Round Table and Camelot.

## Uther Pendragon's magical transformation: Arthur's miraculous conception

Malory follows Geoffrey of Monmouth in supposing the place of Arthur's conception to have been Tintagel, 'Castle of the Narrow Neck', an aptly named ancient stronghold set atop sheer cliffs soaring some 90 metres (295 ft) up from the sea that almost completely surrounds this protruding section of rugged northern Cornish coastline.[2] According to Malory, Uther Pendragon was so consumed with lust for Igraine, the wife of the Duke of Cornwall, that he was willing to pay any price to fulfil his desire. Merlin, therefore, agreed to grant Uther his wish if Uther would grant him his own: the enchanter would transform the king into the very semblance of the duke so that he might have his way with the queen without her knowledge of her lover's true identity; in return, however, the sorcerer demanded that the fruit of that passion conceived that very night in the duke's bed would be disposed with as Merlin saw fit. Conscious only of his desperate need to slake his carnal thirst, Uther agreed to Merlin's terms without compunction.

In accordance with Merlin's demand, the baby born of Igraine from her union with Uther in the semblance of her husband was taken unchristened from his mother's breast and delivered into the hands of the sorcerer, who – in the guise of an old man – took the child, wrapped in costly cloths, from his attendants, two knightly men and two courtly ladies. Merlin then made for the dominions of Sir Ector, who raised the infant prince as his own, and received great rewards from his king for so doing. Arthur, for his part, was raised in complete ignorance of his origin, thinking himself the son of Ector, raised as he was on the milk of that lord's wife.

It so happened that within two years Uther fell into a wasting illness, and his enemies thought to overrun his realm during his feebleness. The vision and wisdom of Merlin forestalled such a catastrophe, however, as the prophet assured the ailing king that, so long as the monarch appeared upon the field of battle, even incapacitated and carried in a litter, his enemies would never defeat Uther's armies. Thus the king went to battle upon a horse-drawn bed, and all came to pass as Merlin had foretold. The king was victorious and returned to London in triumph.

Then the king was struck down to the threshold of death by a horrible malady, and he could not so much as speak for three days and nights; Merlin, however, was equal to this extremity as well; he commanded that all the lords of the realm gather, and he himself would contrive to help the king to speak. The next day before the assembled nobles Merlin asked the king if Arthur, his son, was not his sole and true heir, and this assertion Uther confirmed in the hearing of them all, just before he died.

## The sword in the stone: Arthur's childhood feats

The following years were ones of strife, for although King Uther had proclaimed his son Arthur to be his heir, many others contrived to gain the kingship for themselves, and no one knew, in any case, where the child-prince might be. At length Merlin imposed upon the Archbishop of Canterbury to summon all the lords of Britain to come to London by Christmas, so that Christ in his mercy – he who had

Newell Convers Wyeth, an illustration from Thomas Malory's *The Boy's King Arthur* (1922 edn) showing Merlin taking away the infant Arthur.

Detail from a manuscript, showing the sword being presented to Arthur. The inscription on the stone is: 'Whoever pulls this sword out will be king of the land.'

come to save all mankind – would make known who was rightfully King of Britain, and thus save that realm from further turmoil.

The nobles of the realm therefore gathered that Yuletide in London, as per the command of the archbishop; and so it came to pass that one day, as the congregation of the great church of that city exited after matins and the first Mass of the day, they were all amazed to see in the yard of the church a massive square of stone, seemingly of marble, on the top of which was affixed a steel anvil a foot in height. And plunged deep into that anvil and down into the stone beneath was a great sword of marvellous workmanship, the inscription of which proclaimed that the only man who could unsheathe the naked blade from its scabbard of stone and steel was the true King of Britain. When the archbishop was informed of this wonder, he commanded that none should touch the sword until the High Mass was sung; after the Holy Office was completed, however, many a man who would be king tried his hand at drawing that sword, although none succeeded. It was decided, therefore, that a great tournament would be held in London upon New Year's Day, both so that the true king might be revealed and so that the assembled lords and commons would be present to witness the miracle which would declare their king unto them.

It so happened that Sir Ector had determined to attend the tournament, and with him was his son Sir Kay, who had been knighted just the previous All Hallows' Day; Arthur accompanied them, and served his foster brother Kay as a page. As the party made its way to the fields of combat, Kay realized that he had left his sword at their lodging, and Arthur thus made haste to return there and to seek it for him. Returning to the inn, however, Arthur found it locked, as all had departed to witness the spectacle of the tournament. Determined that his brother should not be without a sword at the contest, Arthur made his way to the churchyard, which he found abandoned by its knight-guardians, who had themselves gone to the competition. Taking the sword easily from the stone, Arthur returned to Kay, who recognized the blade immediately. Kay thought that he might therefore be declared king, but Ector soon deduced the truth, returning to the church with both boys and having each in turn try to remove the blade from its mount. Although Kay and Ector could not shift the sword at all when it sat in the stone, Arthur might put it in and take it out again without effort. Ector and Kay thus knelt before Arthur, much to his discomfiture, and his foster father explained to the young king his true identity and the story of his origins, insofar as he knew it.

The archbishop was then told of this wonder, and Arthur performed the feat again before the assembled lords, none of whom could budge the blade an inch. The jealousy and spite of some of these nobles were so great, however, that they refused to recognize Arthur as their king, and so he repeated his miraculous feat at Candlemas, and at Easter, and again at Pentecost. Finally the common people were so incensed at the delay and the duplicity of the nobles that they declared as a body that Arthur was their king, and that they would slay any man who stood against him. So it was that Arthur was crowned King of Britain.

In addition to sweeping mythic themes, stories concerning Arthur's conception and childhood are rich in folkloric details. For example, the agreement between Uther and Merlin that the infant prince be delivered into the hands of the wizard unchristened clearly recalls the common conceit – repeated by Malory – that the sorcerer was the spawn of the Devil. The infant prince's rich coverlets and journey from royal birth to childhood obscurity before his eventual ascendancy as an earthly sovereign might also be suggestive of an inversion of the life story of the Christ Child, who was born into worldly obscurity but transcended these humble origins to be proclaimed a heavenly prince. Indeed, Merlin's later collusion with the Archbishop of Canterbury to summon all of the squabbling nobles to gather at Christmas to determine their true king explicitly invites an exploration of the relationship between Christ and Arthur, both of whom are clearly messianic figures, and Malory takes some pains to phrase this passage in such a way as to develop the notion of the parallel between the King of Mankind and the rightful King of Britain. Moreover, the ritual transfer of Arthur the suckling babe from the bed of childbirth into the hands of what amounts to an unholy inversion of a godfather is underscored both by the detail that the transfer is effected by two couples – much like the parents and sponsors at a christening – and by the fact that Malory reports that it was Merlin who brought the child to his foster parents, and also who caused the boy to be christened by a holy man, thus taking on himself the dual role of father figure and godfather.

Merlin also took the lead in unveiling Arthur's true identity as king, of course, an episode rich in mythological significance. The young Arthur's ability to remove the sword from the stone – not just once, moreover, but again and again before the assembled lords and commons – clearly manifests an example of what are commonly known as the 'childhood feats' of the hero.[3] Such figures generally are marked as special in a number of ways, not least by their superlative and even superhuman powers, which quite often become apparent in childhood, and sometimes even in infancy. The hero's special status may thus be evident from his earliest days; in the case of the story of the sword in the stone, of course, Arthur does not perform just any miraculous feat. Rather, he completes the specific task destined to identify the true King of Britain, he does it on multiple occasions and he does it in the clear context of the failure of many, many other contestants. This particular episode, then, does not merely recount the marvellous abilities of a given superhuman figure; it also illustrates how this young lad and nascent hero, a stripling not yet even knighted, is able to best a whole range of older, more experienced claimants to the throne, rivals who are decidedly displeased to be supplanted by such a beardless boy. Thus, before proving himself a superlative warrior – although he certainly does so in due course – Arthur is identified as king through an archetypal heroic feat which fairly reverberates with the tones of miracle and magic, an achievement which displays the subtle hand of Merlin in the development and unveiling of Arthur's unique nature.

It was also Merlin, of course, who incited the dying Uther to proclaim publicly that Arthur should succeed him as King of Britain; it was Merlin, too, who conspired to bring all the nobles of the kingdom together at Christmas, and who provided the sword in the stone with which Arthur's identity as this heralded heir was made manifest. Time and again Merlin acts not just as Arthur's mentor and guide, but as an instrument of fate, a kingmaker who facilitates the destiny of his young ward.

Meanwhile, Arthur's childhood in the care of Ector, of whom he believes himself the son, evokes aspects of the archetype of the hero's search for his father. Although fosterage was a common practice in aristocratic and royal households in the Middle Ages and indeed earlier, Arthur's words of dismay when Ector and Kay kneel before him after he has drawn the sword from the stone, as well as his foster father's subsequent response and the young king's eventual joyful reunion with the mother he never knew, all underscore the fact that Arthur had not the least idea of his own real parentage or royal heritage. Obscure origins are a hallmark of the hero, as is the desire to resolve such obscurity, which is often manifested in the hero's quest for his father. Arthur, in Malory's telling, does not overtly seek his father, because his true identity is hidden even from him. After his foster father reveals the truth proclaimed by Arthur's act of pulling the sword from the stone, however, Merlin overtly steps forward into the role of a father figure, both as a mentor and as a shaman guide. It was Merlin, after all, who from the onset acted in the capacity of a spiritual father to Uther's son, first through making Arthur's conception possible in the first place, then consequently by forcing the king to allow him to take upon himself the decision concerning the prince's fosterage; throughout it all, moreover, Merlin assiduously protected his young charge's inheritance.

Indeed, any discussion of the eponymous Arthurian hero's miraculous conception and marvellous childhood feats invites a close examination of the figure who in the first case made such a conception possible and who later acted as the chief guide and mentor to the boy who would be king. Merlin is the nascent hero's shaman guide, the prophet and sorcerer who acts as a conduit between the earthly young Arthur and the otherworldly forces which initially declare the heroic identity and ultimately shape the legendary destiny of the son of Uther's lust and flesh, and the heir to his throne and ambition.

## Merlin: Arthur's shaman guide

'Shamanism' across the globe may be defined broadly as a related collection of spiritual practices and beliefs often gathered in the person of a 'holy healer' of sorts, a visionary spiritual leader who acts as a conduit to spiritual wisdom and the otherworld for his people.[4] Shamans are generally seers, often shape-shifters or associated with totemic animals, and sometimes act as guides to the underworld for the recently deceased. The visionary powers of the shaman may be imparted or transmitted through ecstatic visions and/or a form of sacred madness, through which they permeate the borders of the mundane, workaday waking world to participate in a realm of mythic proportions in which fantastic images and messages may take the form of dreams in order to translate into discernible human dimensions and symbols a higher truth and order of existence. Shamanistic beliefs are widespread throughout the globe, and generally are associated with animistic and numinous traditions, that is, with those cultures that perceive powerful spiritual forces nearly everywhere in the landscape, monuments and objects which surround them.

Although Shamanism was certainly on the wane in mainstream European societies by the time of the High Middle Ages in which Sir Thomas Malory lived, remnants of ancient Celtic and Germanic beliefs, for example, displayed some shamanistic tendencies, and the early Irish and Welsh traditions which gave birth to the Arthurian mythology of the Middle Ages were rich in a demonstrable concern with spiritually imbued sacred rocks, springs, mounds and the like, as well as with magic cauldrons, weapons and other objects virtually

Miniature of Merlin showing a tablet to Arthur and
Guinevere, from an early 14th-century French manuscript.

rendered incandescent by the spiritual power they channel: no
example of this trend is more obvious or well-known than the Grail
itself. The medieval British traditions are also well-supplied with
Shaman figures, spiritual guides and visionary prophets who shape
and control access to the power and truths available through access
to the world of spirits, gods and magic. In all, Merlin is a particularly
well-developed medieval example of the timeless archetype of the
shaman guide.

Merlin as we know him through the lens of *Le Morte Darthur* is
in some ways the culmination of a number of traditions in early
Welsh, Irish and Scottish mythology and folklore in which various
aspects of the shaman are made manifest. Geoffrey of Monmouth
combined a rich narrative tradition which developed around a pseudo-
historical figure known as Myrddin, drawn from the late sixth century,

with Ambrosius Aurelianus, also known as *Emrys Wledig*.[5] This is a Welsh translation of the same name which may be rendered 'Prince Ambrosius', a native British interpretation of the Latin name which may refer to the place this figure earned in the company of the Roman gods through his earthly heroism in his defeat of the rampaging Saxons.

Gildas deemed this figure the last of the true Romano-British heroes. Geoffrey borrowed this apparently factual – if heavily embroidered – fifth-century figure from Nennius and renamed him Merlin Ambrosius; the resultant amalgam is often cited as the progenitor of the figure we know as 'Merlin' from later medieval tradition, as well as many of the facets and adventures associated with that more familiar Merlin, including perhaps most notably the role of the sorcerer who empowers Uther to sate his lust upon Igraine, thereby facilitating the miraculous conception of Arthur himself. Merlin thus emerges in this tradition as a prime example of the shaman guide, in this case combining his archetypal role as seer and mentor with that of a surrogate father figure, in that he literally brings about the very birth of the hero before aiding and shepherding his spiritual charge by means of the shaman's otherworldly powers and prophetic vision.

Merlin in fact plays similar roles in many of the Arthurian narratives which follow Geoffrey of Monmouth, most of which undoubtedly draw upon the *Historia*'s description of this shaman's role in facilitating the very conception of the hero whom he is later to shape, protect and guide. Both supernatural powers and preternatural sight are ascribed to Merlin by Geoffrey as a result of the wizard's purportedly being descended from an incubus, although William of Newburgh takes Geoffrey to task for this claim, which he debunks as theologically ridiculous. Doctrinal niceties aside, Merlin's underworldly origin as the spawn of a devil became a staple element of Arthurian lore, perhaps culminating in the French Vulgate Cycle of the early fourteenth century. This cycle was a set of five prose romances that revolved around Lancelot, the Grail quest, Arthur and Merlin, and which were a great influence upon those Arthurian works that followed, including – most notably in the terms of the present discussion – *Le Morte Darthur*. In the story of the genesis of Merlin described in the school of the Vulgate Cycle, Merlin was conceived of by devils specifically to

Merlin, disguised as a child, standing before King Arthur and his barons.

perform the function of an Antichrist, a wicked intention thwarted by Merlin's mother, whose insistence upon having her child baptized recast this scion of evil into a force for good. Merlin, according to this tradition, was thus granted encyclopaedic knowledge of the past from his infernal father, while he was granted foresight by God as an aspect of his holy conversion.

## Myrddin the mad Welsh poet

The Welsh figure Myrddin, 'Seamount', known in some texts as Gwyllt, or 'Mad', Myrddin, is a poet purported to have lived in the sixth century and rendered a seer through the madness which beset him after the death of his lord, Gwenddolou fab Ceido, a petty king of what was known to the Welsh as the 'Old North', a Welsh-speaking region in what is now the Scottish lowlands.[6] Gwenddolou died at the hands of Peredur and Gwrgi, the sons of Eliffer, at the Battle of Arfderydd in the 570s. This conflict was won by Gwenddolou's enemy Rhydderch Hael, 'Generous Most-honoured Lord', the King of Strathclyde, from whom Myrddin fled into the Scottish wilderness in fear. As the story goes, Myrddin consequently lived in terror of his lord's nemesis for some fifty years, inhabiting treetops and abiding among the wild beasts of the forests. This characterization of Myrddin's exile clearly evokes the 'wild man of the woods' theme, and the madness which is the impetus for his prophetic gifts is a commonplace of shamanistic traditions.

The earliest extant text which references Myrddin is known as the *Armes Prydain*, or 'Prophecy of Britain', a tenth-century cradle of Welsh nationalism which, in two hundred lines of verse, sounds a clarion call to all the Celtic peoples of the British Isles, as well as to the Vikings of Dublin, to unite and to expel the Saxon invaders from Britain.[7] The figure of Myrddin is used almost interchangeably with that of Merlin after the conflation enacted by Geoffrey of Monmouth, although the distinct Welsh flavour of Myrddin is enhanced by a series of texts which link him with the great poet and prophet Taliesin, the apex of which is a dialogue from the twelfth century in which the two seers exchange the hidden wisdom known only to each other. Moreover, the reputation of Myrddin as a poet was so well-developed in the ensuing centuries that anonymous verse was at times ascribed to him, and poems were even occasionally told from his perspective. Indeed, the *Llyfr Du Caerfyrddin* (Black Book of Carmathen), a mid-thirteenth-century Welsh manuscript and a seminal source of Welsh heroic verse, is a prime example of this trend, as it contains a wealth of poems from the previous three centuries, a fair proportion of which purport to give voice to Myrddin himself.

The 'wild man of the woods' motif is also developed in legendary accounts of the Scottish figure Lailoken, in whom, it is generally agreed, one might find the germ of the eponymous wizard described in Geoffrey of Monmouth's mid-twelfth-century *Vita Merlini*.[8] The fact that Lailoken employs his abilities as a seer at the seat of Rhydderch Hael suggests a close association between this figure and that of Myrddin. A late medieval Scottish text further explores the possibilities of such a link by attributing Lailoken's madness to the deaths at the Battle of Arfderydd, deaths for which the Scottish wild man takes responsibility.

## Mad Sweeney: an Irish Myrddin

A similar theme of madness wrought by the horrors of war is evoked in tales surrounding the Irish figure Suibhne Geilt, 'Sweeney the Crazed', a character often compared with Myrddin, especially in the terms of the madness of each. Suibhne is best known from a twelfth-century recounting of an episode drawn from the Cycle of Kings known as *Buile Shuibhne*, the 'Insanity of Sweeney', the third in a triad of stories revolving around the seventh-century Battle of Magh Rath.[9] The first tale sets the scene, while the second details the events of the battle. It is the third story, though, that of the trials and tribulations of Sweeney himself, his mind broken as he wanders the length and breadth of Ireland, that has most captured the imagination of ensuing generations, and that most clearly resonates with the tales of Myrddin and Lailoken, in its setting and events, its evocation of the 'wild man of the woods' motif and its employment of the theme of poetic vision gained through madness.

Although it has many of the earmarks of a pagan narrative, Sweeney's experience in this version of his story is framed by his initial rejection and ultimate acceptance of the new faith of Christ. As the King of Dál nAraide in the east of what is now Northern Ireland, Sweeney attempted to prevent the proselytizing of St Ronan within his borders, a recalcitrant attitude which resulted in a pair of cataclysmic curses from the cleric, as well as his unrelenting enmity. When Sweeney first charged out of his hall to confront Ronan, the queen attempted to stop him, ripping the robe from her husband's body in the process; Sweeney then wrenched the priest's psalter from his hands and cast it into the nearby lake, although he was called to the Battle of Magh Rath before he had the opportunity to strike down the preacher himself. Praising God for his deliverance, Ronan responded to this unprovoked assault by prophesying that Sweeney should go through the world as naked as he was when he attacked the saint. Later, after the saint had tried in vain to bring about peace between the warring parties, the king cast a spear at the priest which shattered as it struck the holy man's bell. Ronan responded to this onslaught by cursing the king to fly through Ireland as did the shaft of his spear, as well as decreeing that Sweeney would himself die at the point of just such a missile.

Turning from the face of his antagonist in contempt, Sweeney attempted to rush into the fray upon the battlefield, only to be overcome by a kind of fit. Shaking wildly like a nervous bird, Sweeney found himself literally flitting about from spot to spot along the ground, for all the world as though he were about to take flight into the air. Finally he sprang from the earth, taking refuge in the branches of a yew tree – a highly symbolic perch, as this tree has long been associated in the Celtic imagination with immortality, fertility, magic and even ecstatic visions. Sweeney flew from one such tree to another, unable to save his allies from defeat in the battle or even to return to his own kith and kin. Flying about the island in a state of frantic and largely incoherent exile, Sweeney embodied the very image of the madman of the wilderness; he even lived for a time in Glenn Bolcain, Ireland's famous Valley of the Insane. Mad though he was, Sweeney was never abandoned by his loyal companion Loingsechan, who played the part of messenger between the mad sovereign and his family and friends, or by his wife, Eorann, who refused to repudiate her union with her husband even when Sweeney himself attempted to persuade her to do so.

A crucial element of the curse of insanity in this narrative illustrates the link in shaman-like figures between the gifts of poetic or prophetic vision and the costs thereof; in archetypal terms, the gods served by shamans often give with one hand while they take with the other. Sweeney's madness, although in most ways leaving him utterly bereft of the creature comforts and human relationships of the life which he had known, did impart unto him poetic insight, a gift manifested in several transcendent poems attributed to the mad king during the course of the text. Yet even during periods of stability Sweeney was pursued by the antagonism of Ronan, who continually entreated the Lord to prevent the pagan tyrant from returning to his home and his senses, from which vantage he might renew his attacks upon the Holy Church. Sweeney later died quite literally in the embrace of that Church, speared by the jealous husband of the cook at a monastery which had given him shelter. Just as the good monks had given poor Crazed Sweeney bodily sustenance, however, they had likewise fed his soul with Holy Writ and the Lord's Supper, so the mad king died in the faith he had once persecuted. A less dramatic figure sometimes touched upon in discussions of the role of the shaman guide in medieval Irish literature is Sencha mac Ailella of the Ulster Cycle, himself a royal poet, judge and the great hero Cúchulainn's teacher. Thus, like Sweeney, Lailoken and Myrddin,

Sencha is another character who has often been associated with the figure of Merlin in the Arthurian canon.

## The sorcerer's weakness: Nenive and the demise of Merlin

Vital catalyst and surrogate father figure though he is, Merlin exits the stage very early in the version of events recounted in *Le Morte Darthur*.[10] Malory describes Merlin's demise as a foreseen but inexorable fate at the hands of Nenive – also known as Vivien, as well as several variations of both names – who was, according to the passage concerning her beguiling of Merlin in *Le Morte Darthur*, one of the damsels of the Lady of the Lake. On the other hand, in Malory's account of Arthur's mortal wound and his subsequent translation to Avalon, Nenive is identified as the principal Lady of the Lake, the wife of Sir Pelleas and a helpful ally to King Arthur.

According to Malory, Merlin became enamoured of a young maiden who came to the court of King Arthur in the company of King Pellinore. This was Nenive, and Merlin was so besotted with her that he followed her everywhere and schemed to take her virginity. Nenive, meanwhile, though she found Merlin's attentions tiresome, encouraged his attendance upon her until she had learned all that she might from him concerning his gifts of magic and foresight. Through this very same second sight Merlin was aware of his own impending demise, but he was so infatuated with Nenive that he could not control his actions. The enchanter went to King Arthur, therefore, and informed his lord of the doom that was soon to put him into the earth, and gave the ruler the benefit of his gift of prophecy in many other matters as well, and especially concerning Arthur's sword and scabbard, which Merlin begged the king to keep ever near to his person, as he was destined to lose them through the agency of a woman whom he trusted above all others. Although King Arthur asked his old counsellor if the sorcerer might not through his subtle arts manage to cheat his destiny, Merlin, resigned to the power of providence, answered that what was to be would be, and soon thereafter departed from the court for the last time.

Nenive also went forth, and Merlin continued to connive to be alone with her, in the vain hope of making love to her. Lamenting that she feared that he might achieve his wicked ends through his sorcery, the maiden forced her devoted admirer to swear that he would cast no spell upon her. Merlin and Nenive then travelled together to the kingdom of Benwick, and eventually they found their way to Cornwall; all the while the wizard instructed the ingénue in the ways of his craft, and showed to her many wonderful sights. Merlin's continued assaults upon Nenive's maidenhead, however, grew too annoying for the girl to endure; moreover, she feared him as the scion of an infernal incubus. Thus the maiden contrived a plot to rid herself of Merlin and his attentions forever. Having been told by the warlock of a wondrous marvel conceived through magic which was formed within a stone hidden beneath a mighty boulder, Nenive convinced the old fool to go within the cavity beneath the boulder so that he might recount to her the wonders he found therein; once Merlin was within this stony enclosure, however, Nenive cast a spell such as those Merlin himself might have shown her, and the result of this sorcery was that the wizard was imprisoned beneath the boulder, from which narrow cell he could not escape, despite all his vaunted powers. Nenive went her way then, but Merlin languished in that place ever after.

The wider tradition that informed the story of Merlin contained in *Le Morte Darthur* offers several variations on the theme of the demise of Arthur's sorcerer, prophet and shaman guide. In the early thirteenth-century Vulgate *Estoire de Merlin*, for example, the enchanter is held captive in a tower cell by a devoted Niniane (another form of the Nenive figure), who offers him her love and designs his incarceration merely to reserve his undivided attention for herself. Few authors allow the old magician such a pleasant retirement, however. In other versions of the story Merlin's prison is a cave or a tomb, as in the post-Vulgate *Suite du Merlin*, in which the infatuated warlock meets his death after being sealed and left to die inside the enchanted grave of two lovers. In still another variation on the theme of Merlin's imprisonment, the maiden Vivien seals the magician within the trunk of a mighty oak tree within the Forest of Brocéliande in Brittany. In some iterations of this narrative theme the wizard ultimately dies as a result of his captivity, while in others he is trapped in the living

This cavern, located almost directly below the island courtyard
which houses the Great Hall of the 13th-century castle on Tintagel,
is accessible from the beach when the tide is out and has been known
as Merlin's Cave at least since the time of Alfred, Lord Tennyson.

death of eternal entombment. In almost every case Nenive or some
related female figure entices and entrances – and ultimately ensnares
and entraps – a besotted Merlin.

Her unequivocal identification with the Lady of the Lake, as
well as with Morgan le Fay (to whom we are about to turn) and with
Arthur's journey to Avalon, all clearly mark the figure often known
as Nenive as a denizen of the otherworld, with magical powers in
this world and the ability to move between these spheres of existence
at will. A fairy maiden of such provenance and abilities provides both
an appropriate foil for and an irresistible attraction to a shamanistic
figure such as Merlin, whose very role in the Arthurian cycle is
founded upon the gifts he has derived from his ability to permeate
the shroud between this ordinary plane of existence and that of the
otherworld. His lust for Nenive thus may serve to symbolize his
unquenchable thirst for forbidden knowledge of and unlimited access
to that alternate world of wonders. A discussion of the episode of

the besotted Merlin's undoing through the wiles of Nenive leads us naturally to the figure of Morgan le Fay, the great femme fatale of the Arthurian tradition.

## Morgan le Fay: shadows of an ancient goddess in the face of a medieval witch

Malory develops the theme of Arthur's treacherous and powerful half-sisters, female figures of great physical attraction and sexual licentiousness coupled with dangerous magical powers and a desire to dominate the King of Britain. Any reader with a passing familiarity with the Morrigna or other medieval Irish and Welsh manifestations of ancient Celtic war goddesses will suspect that Malory's depiction of Arthur's sisters may in some measure resonate with the ancient battle goddesses who condemned those destined to fall, granted victory to their favourites and often marked the greatest of heroes – especially those destined for kingship – by mating with or in any event attempting to seduce these mightiest of warriors.[11] While this trope is absent from Geoffrey of Monmouth's *Historia*, references such as that in the *Vita Merlini* to one Morgen, the chief sorceress of a coven, make clear that the femme fatale of *Le Morte Darthur* was not created by Malory out of whole cloth, and in fact draws upon a number of medieval and perhaps even ancient sources.

Rather like the Morrigna of the Irish tradition, it might be argued that the three half-sisters Malory attributes to Arthur – Elaine, Morgan and Morgause – all represent varying faces of the same ancient archetypal goddess.[12] Malory does not tell us much of Elaine but that she was wedded to King Nentres of Garlot, so there is little obvious evidence in this text of her mythic provenance, although incidence of triplism is noteworthy in the context of any narrative influenced by Celtic mythological traditions; thus it may well be significant that Malory names three half-sisters of Arthur, as well as claiming that three was the number of ladies in the barge which carried the fallen king to Avalon to heal him of his mortal wound.

## Maiden, wife and crone: Celtic goddesses in Arthurian robes

Considering the ancient Celtic trope of the triple goddess, as well as the related tripartite concept of maiden, wife and crone, it might be suggested that Elaine's main function in this text is to underscore the mythic identities of her two sisters. Indeed, if one were to cast Elaine as the 'maiden', or innocent, in this schema, the purposes of the other sisters in the text might be clarified: Morgause is, on one level, something of a 'wife' to Arthur, serving as she does as the mother of her brother's incestuous bastard; moreover, Morgan is clearly something of a 'crone', a witch who functions as the death-dealing enemy of Arthur and who at the last serves as his psychopomp, or 'spirit guide' to the otherworld. Indeed, Morgan's very designation as *Le Fay*, 'the Fairy', invites a discussion of how the otherworld of the fairy realm is manifested and to be comprehended in the context of the world depicted in *Le Morte Darthur*.

Although we may not know much for certain about Elaine, there is – independent of any theory relying upon conjecture concerning the ancient Celtic mythic reflex of triplism – much to say concerning Morgan and Morgause, Arthur's other two half-sisters. Morgan is Arthur's sibling in *Le Morte Darthur*, but she is also his sworn enemy, often – as notably in *Sir Gawain and the Green Knight* – depicted as something of a hag and a harridan who makes no pretence about the love lost between her and her royal brother; in Malory's telling, however, his sisters are still comely, if all the more deadly, and are also often sexually voracious. Morgan is, in any event, a healer as well as a witch, and in various other texts these attributes of hers are highlighted. In Hartmann von Aue's *Erec*, for example, an analogous figure known as Famurgan bequeaths unto Arthur a talisman of healing, although this power – along with a host of other magical properties – are in this text credited to the witch's compact with Satan.

In the mid-twelfth-century *Vita Merlini*, however, Morgan's abilities as a healer are more clearly developed in a context which suggests that this figure may well have been derived from a pre-Christian Celtic goddess.[13] Here Morgan is described as the chief of nine magical sisters, witches who rule the fairy realm of the *Insula Avallonia*, the 'Island of Apples', as it was described by William of

Frank William Warwick Topham, *Voyage of King Arthur
and Morgan Le Fay to the Isle of Avalon*, 1888, oil on canvas.

Malmesbury, that mystical land which ultimately will become known
as Avalon. This queen of the otherworld is also a shape-changer, an
attribute suggestive of her role as a shaman guide who may permeate
the boundaries between worlds. In this case, however, Arthur is
brought to her, and so she does not serve directly as a psychopomp.
She does cause Arthur to be brought to her, though, and is confident
that she can heal his wounds, given ample time. Many also have
identified Morgan with Argante, the fairy queen of Avalon in
Layamon's *Brut*, whose healing powers would make Arthur whole.

It is often suggested that aspects of the figure of Morgan le Fay
were drawn from the medieval Welsh Modron, who herself ultimately
derived from the ancient Gaulish 'mother goddess' Matrona, who
was associated specifically with the River Marne, and with life-giving
and healing forces in general.[14] Although her powers in *Le Morte
Darthur* might be thought in and of themselves to be suggestive of
such a divine origin, an even more compelling link between Morgan
and Modron concerns the husband and offspring of each figure.
Although primarily remembered as the lamenting mother of the
kidnapped Mabon, especially as that tale is remembered in the Welsh
*Culhwch and Olwen*, Modron was also the mother of Owain ab Urien,

who was fathered by Urien Rheged. Modron appeared to Urien in the context of the 'washer woman at the ford' motif, which in itself would tend to associate her closely with death figures and warrior goddesses such as the Irish Morrigna. Moreover, this mysterious young woman explicitly identified herself to Urien as a daughter of Annwfn, which is to say as a denizen of the otherworld.

## The medieval Morgan: the making of a witch

Morgan, according to Malory, was first sequestered in a convent, where (ironic though it may seem to modern readers) she proved herself an apt pupil of the black arts. Later, our narrator informs us, this budding young witch was married off to King Uriens of Gore, whom she was later prevented from killing only by the timely physical intervention of their son Sir Uwain, who himself calls her a demon of this world. In *Le Morte Darthur* Morgan is ever the enemy of Arthur, a consequence which seems to be the explicable result of her hatred for Uther Pendragon, who supplanted Morgan's own father in her mother Igraine's bed. Her enmity for her half-brother is manifested in a number of ways, perhaps most notably when she arranges in secret for his sword, Excalibur, to be stolen away and then replaced with a false and brittle copy. She then ensured that Arthur might do battle with Accolon of Gaul, to whom she had secreted the real Excalibur.

Arthur's ability to withstand the onslaught of his own charmed blade underscores his superlative abilities and his identity as a hero of supernatural proportions. In the end, however, it was only the magical intercession of the Lady of the Lake which allowed Arthur to reclaim his sword at a crucial moment and thus to best his opponent. Morgan subsequently crept into her brother's chamber while he slept and, although she was too frightened to take the sword itself, she stole its scabbard, the marvellous properties of which included the quality of protecting the bearer from being badly wounded or shedding blood. When Arthur pursued her, Morgan cast this charmed sheath into a lake, so that it would be lost to her brother; she then transformed herself and her attendants into stones so that they might elude capture.

Later Morgan sent her brother a mantle, the most lavish and costly robe anyone at court had ever seen. The young damsel who presented it to him claimed that Morgan had sent it in earnest of her desire to be reconciled with her brother, and this gift and words pleased Arthur very much indeed. Before the king had the chance to don the mantle, however, Nenive (the Lady of the Lake) came to Arthur and beseeched him to speak privately with her. As soon as they were alone the lady revealed to Arthur that she feared that the robe was a danger to him, and she begged him not to wear it, nor to let any of his retainers do so, until she who had delivered the mantle had worn it. Agreeing to be guided by the Lady of the Lake, King Arthur summoned Morgan's messenger and commanded her to try on the gift she had brought. Although the young maiden tried to demur, claiming that such a gift would not befit her, the king insisted.

The warning of the Lady of the Lake was then proved well founded, for as soon as the maid was covered in the garment she dropped dead, and her body was reduced to ashes by the potent and evil properties of that fell cloak. So wrathful was Arthur over this further proof of Morgan's treachery that he banished her son Sir Uwain from his court, because he had no way of assaying the loyalty of the spawn of such a vile creature. However, Arthur knew Morgan's husband, King Uriens, to be the object of the witch's plots as well, and so he did not dismiss him. Arthur's dismissal of Uwain caused Gawain to leave the court as well, and so the ill will of Morgan struck at Arthur again through the suspicion it aroused in the king's own breast.

It is noteworthy that Morgan does not limit her attacks upon her half-brother to attempts to disarm, unman or slay him. Indeed, as her role in *Sir Gawain and the Green Knight* makes clear, one of the primary ways in which Morgan's enmity towards Arthur manifests itself is through her desire to shame and humiliate him, most especially by terrorizing his wife Guinevere, which is her purpose in *Sir Gawain*. Morgan often seeks to dishonour Guinevere as well, and this theme is perhaps most eloquently expressed in the episode of the Golden Horn of Fidelity, which discusses one of Morgan's attempts to publicly embarrass Arthur's queen for her affair with Lancelot. It is also of note that this episode draws an explicit reference to this liaison into the context of the other great adulterous coupling of the

Edmund Leighton, *The End of the Song*, 1902, oil on canvas.

Arthurian canon, that of Tristan and Isolt (known in Malory as Tristram and Isode).

Malory opens his version of the tale by relating that Morgan had arranged for a certain knight to deliver unto Arthur a lovely drinking horn chased with gold. The magical property of this vessel was such that, although a faithful wife could drink from it without mishap, any noblewoman who had betrayed her husband's trust could not sip from it without spilling the whole of its contents. Morgan sent this horn to her half-brother in hatred of Guinevere and in knowledge of the queen's indiscretions with Lancelot. It came to pass, however, that the knight delivering the horn came under the power of Sir Lamorak, who forced him – in fear of his life – to deliver the horn instead to King Mark, out of Lamorak's own enmity for Tristram. In the end Isode and a hundred ladies of the court of Cornwall raised the horn to their lips, and Mark and all but four of the husbands of those ladies found themselves publicly marked as cuckolds by the brimming liquid spilling down over their wives. Although King Mark determined to burn all these adulteresses, his nobles would not have any lady so condemned because of an enchanted object created through sorcery by a witch known to be both evil and ever the enemy of true love. Thus Isode and her faithless companions were saved from the flames, Morgan le Fay was more reviled than ever and Sir Tristram was determined to be avenged upon Lamorak, though they later battled to a draw and thus were reconciled.

On another occasion Morgan used Tristram himself to manifest her mockery of her half-brother, Arthur, and his wife, Guinevere. At a tournament at the Hard Roche, Tristram appeared incognito, his only identifying device being that on his shield, which had been given to him by Morgan. This shield depicted the figure of a knight standing with each foot on either of two heads, one that of a king and the other of a queen. Tristram fought throughout that tournament without revealing who he really was, and thus left those who had seen him to wonder at the import of his shield.

## Arthur's sister-wife: Morgause, mother of Mordred

The third of Arthur's half-sisters in *Le Morte Darthur*, Morgause, plays a significant thematic role which has vital archetypal significance regarding the king's identity as a hero. In Malory's telling of the tales of Arthur, Morgause is the wife of King Lot of Orkney and the mother of Gawain and his brothers, who all become loyal retainers of King Arthur, as well as the mother of Mordred, the catalyst who brings about the destruction of Arthur's fellowship and kingship. As the mother of both Gawain and Mordred, Morgause takes on the role played by Anna in some earlier narratives. Although Malory was not the first to attribute Mordred's birth to an unholy, incestuous union between Arthur and one of his half-sisters – the Vulgate Cycle, for example, discusses Mordred's origin in similar terms – the development of the theme of Mordred as Arthur's antithesis, an anti-hero bastard quite literally spawned in the throes of the most sinful and repugnant sexual desire, is particularly well developed in *Le Morte Darthur*.

Indeed, although he follows Geoffrey of Monmouth and others in casting Mordred as an unrepentant villain, Malory's handling of Arthur's moment of incestuous lust with Morgause, the ensuing evil issue of that tryst and Merlin's interpretation of the affair all serve to develop Mordred into a living icon of Arthur's sin and the vehicle for the divine retribution for that sin which will deal Arthur his mortal blow, send him on a barge to an ambiguous otherworldly fate and end the golden age of his reign. Morgause and Mordred, in *Le Morte Darthur*, are not simply the slatternly sister and the incestuous child of Arthur, nor are they simply evil for evil's sake; rather, they are emblems of the hero's flaws and susceptibility to the dictates of a destiny he can neither see nor understand. Thus Morgause and her spawn serve as symbolic figures which represent the human weakness and vanity that cause the hero to transgress, however unknowingly, against the inflexible laws of God, and – rather like Oedipus – thus to seal his own doom. Fate is inexorable for us all, and the hero's fall is necessarily more precipitous and dramatic than that of an ordinary man, functioning as it does not simply as an individual end, but much more importantly as a signifier of every mortal's eventual demise.

## The great quest of Arthurian myth: the search for the Grail in Malory

In Malory's telling of the tale of the *Sangrail*, or 'Holy Grail', the quest for the Cup of Christ is transformed from the more theologically complex moral exemplum of its French source – the Grail quest volume from the monumental thirteenth-century Vulgate Cycle – into essentially a dual heroic quest. In this tale the saintly Galahad ultimately achieves his objective while the concurrent noble failure of Lancelot, rather than merely offering the didactic lesson concerning the wages of sin suggested by its source, is transformed into the emblematic failing of a hero for the flawed and sinful. Thus Lancelot is wrought into a protagonist whose very imperfections make inspirational the fact that he comes so close to the forbidden objective.

## Galahad: Malory's sanctified Grail hero

Although Perceval was the innocent-hearted Grail knight of the tradition following Chrétien de Troyes, this function was appropriated in the Vulgate Cycle by Galahad, and Malory also assigns him this role. Galahad's name is rendered by some as *Gwalch Cad*, Welsh for 'Hawk [of] Battle', even though there is no clear reference to such a character in the Welsh canon.[15] Like Arthur himself, Galahad is a hero whose unusual origins include a miraculous conception wrought through an enchantment of deception. In this tale, however, it is the male lover, no less a figure than Lancelot himself, who is bewitched so that he will lie with a woman he believes to be his beloved Guinevere.

Playing Merlin to her mistress's Uther, Brisen – the maid in waiting of Elaine of Corbenic and one of the most powerful witches of her time – used her magic to convince Lancelot that Elaine was in fact Guinevere; Galahad was the fruit of the union conceived through this beguilement. It was likewise through Brisen's magic that Lancelot both went mad and eventually was healed through the power of the Grail. Duping the knight a second time, Brisen again led Lancelot to an Elaine whom he once again believed to be Guinevere. When the queen learned of her chosen knight's second indiscretion with her rival, however, she spurned Lancelot, and thus he lost his mind. Brisen later made amends to the knight by placing him under an enchantment of slumber until he could be brought to the Grail and healed.

Elaine of Corbenic was the daughter of King Pelles, known as the 'Maimed King' because he was wounded through his thighs when he attempted to draw from its scabbard the Sword of David forbidden to all but Galahad. Pelles was the King of Corbenic, a stronghold built, if one were to give credence to the thirteenth-century *Estoire del Saint Graal*, to house the Grail. Indeed, according to the false etymology provided to validate this account, *Corbenic* was said to be Chaldean for 'Sacred Vessel'.[16]

Galahad's heritage, said to extend to the Royal House of David, also serves to emphasize his identity as a heroic figure of special note.[17] Moreover, Malory takes pains to underscore the thematic resonance between Galahad and Christ, as he does, for instance, in his description of the celestial voice which prophesied to Solomon

Miniature of Galahad, with Perceval and Bors, before King
Arthur, joining the halves of the broken sword.

concerning the last scion of his line, who would remain chaste and
be as mighty as Joshua. Although the immediate context suggests
that this descendant of the House of David would be Christ, the text
later clarifies that this prophecy referred to Galahad. Moreover,
Guinevere herself, recognizing Galahad as the son of Lancelot shortly
after the young knight had appeared at the Court of King Arthur,
noted that Galahad was but nine degrees removed from Christ.

Two marvellous possessions, the Sword of David and the Shield
of Evelake, also indicate Galahad's status as the pure Grail knight
drawn from a biblical pedigree. Since Galahad was of the lineage of
David, and since he was the last of that house and pure in his body,
he was the only knight able to wield the Sword of David, which he
found upon the Ship of Solomon; Galahad's grandfather had attempted
to draw this same sword upon this same ship, much to his lasting
torment. The original girdle created to hold this sword was fashioned
by the wife of Solomon, and the sister of Perceval wove its replacement

out of strands of her own hair. Galahad also acquired a shield destined for him which no other man might carry without placing himself in grave peril. The shield was in the possession of King Evelake of Sarras, who was converted by Joseph of Arimathea. Josephus, the son of Joseph of Arimathea, imparted onto this shield virtues of great holiness when he let the blood of his nose flow upon it in a stream which could not be stemmed. Moving his hand across the crimson flood upon the surface of the shield, Josephus made the sign of the cross, which was the ensign which ever after marked that shield.

As we saw in our discussion of the legendary treasures of Avalon in Chapter Two, Galahad is also marked as the knight destined to achieve the Grail quest by his ability to sit upon the Siege Perilous in the company of the Knights of the Round Table.[18] Accompanied by Sir Bors and Sir Perceval, Galahad ultimately achieves a miraculous vision of the Grail wherein an act of literal transubstantiation takes place: Jesus Christ himself appears out of the Eucharist within the holy vessel, explaining to Galahad that the chalice is none other than the dish wherein he himself was served lamb upon Easter Day, a reference to the Last Supper which emphasizes the role of the Eucharist in embodying the body of Christ, who is the Lamb of God. Jesus then instructs Galahad to depart for the city of Sarras, where he is to become king, with the sacred vessel and in the company of none but Bors and Perceval. Before leaving, however, Galahad is instructed to take some blood from the bleeding lance with which to anoint and thus heal the body of the Maimed King.

Galahad does as commanded by his Saviour and goes to Sarras, where he eventually succeeds the king. Indeed, upon the death of the former sovereign a heavenly voice commands that the people take the youngest of the three knights of Arthur as their lord, and this they do. Every day henceforth Galahad and his companions come to worship before the holy vessel, which he orders to be encased within a jewel-encrusted reliquary. One day, after Galahad has been reigning in the city of Sarras for fully a year, he and his two comrades are granted a vision of a holy man in the semblance of a bishop, surrounded by the angelic chorus, saying Mass. The three knights watch in awe until the moment comes for the consecration of the Host, at which point the officiant calls to Galahad to come forth to behold that vision which he had most desired to see. Trembling with the ecstasy which grips the fleshly in the presence of true spiritual power, Galahad declares that, having seen the Grail with his own eyes, he wishes nothing more than to exchange his earthly home for that of his heavenly father.

Galahad then accepts the body of Christ, which is extended to him by the bishop, who reveals himself to be none other than Josephus, the son of Joseph of Arimathea. Josephus was chosen for this role, he said, because he was like Galahad both in that he had beheld the wonders of the Grail and in that he had kept his body pure. Kissing his companions farewell and sending through them his greetings to Lancelot, his father, Galahad then gives up the ghost, ascending to heaven in the midst of a retinue of angels. Thus the story of Galahad ends with a dramatic apotheosis of the hero, through which the flesh of man is wrought into a spiritual form like unto that of the heavenly creatures. This is an appropriate end for a Grail episode framed by this act of apotheosis and Christ's appearance in the bread of the Mass during the initial vision of the Grail, when the spiritual material of the divine was wrought into the bread of this world. Thus the apotheosis of Galahad provides a moving counterpoint to the literal act of Transubstantiation through which the purest of knights was granted a vision of the bread of communion miraculously transformed into Jesus Christ himself.

## Lancelot: Malory's flawed Arthurian hero

Presented in Malory as a great but significantly flawed hero who is unworthy of achieving the culminating vision of the Grail Quest, the Lancelot of *Le Morte Darthur* still manifests a number of attributes drawn from the very earliest sources concerning this figure. Although in his earliest appearance in Chrétien de Troyes' *Erec* Lancelot is, we are told, the third best of all the knights, he rises in the estimation of that same author in the work dedicated to him, which is generally known by the title the *Knight of the Cart*. In what has sometimes been seen as an exaggeration of the theme of courtly love to parodic extremes, the Lancelot of this work is such a loyal lover to Guinevere that he will gladly suffer any humiliation for her sake. Indeed, the reference to the cart in the alternate title to this romance of *Lancelot* underscores the central debasement of the hero's ordeal: in order to ascertain the whereabouts of his beloved queen, Lancelot is willing to ride in a cart driven by a dwarf; such a conveyance was associated with the transporting of criminals to the gallows, and thus the knight's honour is irretrievably blotted by this selfless act of love, which sets the tone for the lover's travails throughout this romance.

Perhaps most notable for the introduction of the theme of the forbidden love between Lancelot and Guinevere which will play such a central role in the development of the later Arthurian tradition in general and of *Le Morte Darthur* in particular, the romance of the *Knight of the Cart* also agrees with other early sources concerning the otherworldly origin of this hero, which explains why he is known as Lancelot du Lac. Indeed, Chrétien's text agrees with the *Lanzelet* of Ulrich von Zatzikhoven that Lancelot was raised in the realm of a water fairy, an interesting coincidence of detail considering the fact that, although *Lanzelet* is of slightly later date than the *Knight of the Cart*, Ulrich seems to have worked from an independent source, suggesting that the tales of Lancelot might have circulated widely before the time of Chrétien.[19] The Vulgate *Lancelot* refines the story of the hero's origin, identifying the knight's water sprite foster mother as none other than the Lady of the Lake, who is conflated in this source with Ninianne, the nemesis of Merlin. Although Malory does not recount this version of Lancelot's origin, he does allude to related details of the narrative at least twice, when the hero is first mentioned as a boy, and later when we are told that he was confirmed Sir Lancelot du Lac by the Lady of the Lake.

Lancelot du Lac is, of course, generally assumed to be the most quintessentially French character within the entire Arthurian canon; he is identified as French, and his name is explicitly French in origin. Moreover, Lancelot first appears in the French vernacular narrative verse of Chrétien de Troyes in his late twelfth-century *Erec*, and shortly thereafter merits an eponymous romance by the same author. In addition, the Lancelot material within the early thirteenth-century French Vulgate Cycle was highly influential upon Malory's development of the character which has been said to be central to *Le Morte Darthur*, and which many have seen as that author's literary reflection of himself as a flawed yet noble hero.

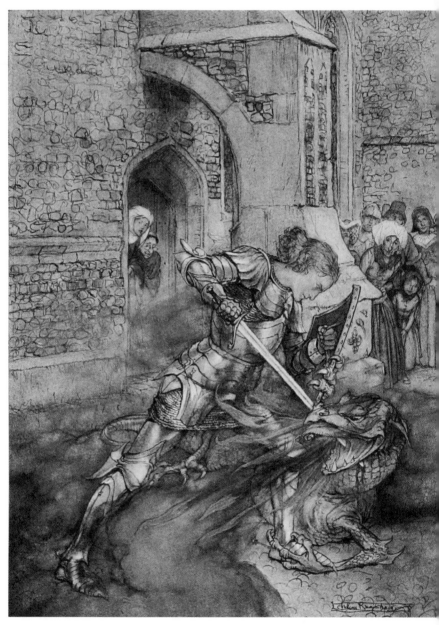

An Arthur Rackham illustration from *The Romance of King Arthur and his Knights of the Round Table*.

Lancelot's Gallic provenance acknowledged, it is worth mentioning that some have seen in this figure a medieval French manifestation of a venerable Celtic god.[20] This suggestion seems even more viable in the light of the fact that Chrétien's *Lancelot* engages Celtic themes. Indeed, a related line of thinking establishes Meleagant – the evil knight in Chrétien's text who spirits the queen away from under the very noses of the court of King Arthur – as Melwas. The latter features in Caradoc's early twelfth-century account of the life of St Gildas as the Welsh 'ruler of death', whose abduction of Guinevere represents an evocation of the Celtic trope of the kidnapped wife who is secreted away to the otherworld by a supernatural captor.[21]

## The barge to Avalon: Arthur's death, journey to the otherworld and apotheosis

In his telling of the story of Arthur's removal to Avalon, Malory explicitly refuses to state whether or not Arthur remains alive, or if he will return once more; he does not, however, repudiate this belief,

James Archer, *The Death of King Arthur*, c. 1860, oil on panel.

which he reports as current in the Isle of Britain, although he does state that Arthur's life here in this world was transformed. The fate of the king is, in any case, ambiguous in *Le Morte Darthur*. Having informed us of his intention to return Excalibur to the Lady of the Lake because his own life was ebbing quickly, and even after the doleful words of his sister upon the barge that they had tarried too long and the wound upon his head had become too cold, Arthur tells Bedivere that he seeks Avalon to be healed; however, he does not state that he anticipates physical healing, or that he will indeed return again. Later Bedivere does come upon a holy hermit who has recently interred a nobleman, and surmises that the grave is Arthur's.

Still, Malory seems determined not to provide a clear answer in this regard, and this ambiguity is emphasized by the epitaph he cites at the end of the passage concerning Bedivere and the hermit: many men, Malory tells us, claim that the grave of Arthur is marked by words proclaiming him the king once, and the king yet again to be. Any mention of Avalon certainly evokes the otherworld, and Arthur's journey there – however slim the hope of his return – smacks of the hero's journey to the otherworld, especially given that he travels in the company of three figures so clearly drawn from the ranks of ancient goddesses and fairy figures.[22] In addition to Malory's rather lukewarm acknowledgement of the tradition of the 'once and future king', several sources explicitly mention the widespread belief that Arthur may return, including those of Wace and Layamon, as well as the late twelfth-century *Vera historia de morte Arthuri*. This tradition of the great mortal king who will conquer death through his sojourn in the otherworld and then return to his people in their hour of need quite clearly resonates with the mythic archetype of the hero's return from the otherworld and apotheosis.

## Mordred: Malory's inverted (and perverted?) Arthurian anti-hero

In early Welsh records such as the *Annales Cambriae*, Mordred's previous incarnation Medraut is neither overtly evil nor even necessarily Arthur's foe.[23] The concept of this figure as irredeemably evil develops rather quickly as the tradition progresses, however. The

Welsh Triads are sometimes ambiguous on this count, but Triad 54 describes in detail the analogous figure Medrawd's churlish behaviour, noting that he behaved piggishly at Arthur's court at Celliwig, devouring every morsel of food and slurping down every drop of drink before insulting Guinevere and challenging Arthur's honour by dragging the queen from her high seat and publicly striking her.[24] It is Geoffrey of Monmouth who first offers the twist of Mordred's treacherous seizure of Arthur's throne, as well as the concomitant and licentious liaison with Arthur's queen, a sordid detail that – in addition to the tawdry motive of lust – may perhaps suggest an evocation of the ancient right of kingship to be won by entering into sexual union with the Sovereignty figure. The Vulgate Cycle gives us the Mordred who is the ill-conceived seed of Arthur begotten upon his own half-sister. This Mordred is, among other vile attributes, notable for how very much his strapping, blond good looks belie his corrupt, nasty character, which is proven by his deeds to be that of a demon.[25] This is the Mordred bequeathed to Malory, a devil of sorts who is developed in *Le Morte Darthur* to the point at which his character becomes quite literally the portrait of an anti-hero, a larger than life and somewhat allegorical character who is branded as particularly noteworthy in the worst of all possible ways from the very moment of his illicit conception.[26] Indeed, the story of Mordred's life manifests several twisted aspects which might well be termed 'anti-archetypes'.

This anti-hero's unusual origin stems from perverted, incestuous parentage, a legacy which led the bastard Mordred's own father to attempt to kill him. When Arthur realized that he had lain with his own sibling and that she had given birth to a son, he attempted to answer for his sin by putting the child to death. To ensure that he caught the correct infant in his murderous trap, he commanded, in a macabre inversion of the Slaughter of the Innocents theme, that all the babies born that day be cast to the savage mercies of the sea. Miraculously emerging, like an Arthurian infant Moses, unscathed from this ordeal, the newborn Mordred was once again marked with the imprimatur of the supernatural. Found by a good and honest man, Mordred was raised in obscurity until the age of fourteen, when he was brought to the court of King Arthur.

Perhaps Malory's most significant emendation to his sources in his account of Mordred's incestuous birth and Arthur's ill-fated attempt to slay his bastard son concerns the fate of the innocents, who survive in the earlier account; in Malory's telling, however, they perish, which causes much grief throughout the kingdom, as well as ill will towards Merlin, who is blamed in this affair because it was he who advised Arthur to pursue this course of action. In addition to any other reasons for this change, however, it is clear that Malory's version evokes the story of the Slaughter of the Innocents, although surely we are to see in the infant Mordred an inversion of the Baby Jesus, an Antichrist who stands in opposition to Arthur, who for all of his sins is clearly the Christ figure of the cycle of stories which bears his name.

The concept of casting children adrift in a pilotless boat is not unique to the Arthurian tradition; indeed, exposing the children of incest in such a way is something of a medieval commonplace, and this theme seems to have had some relationship to historical realities: there is in fact reference to such a practice under Irish law. The theory seems to have been that the fate of such children of sinful unions was best left in the hands of God. The theme of the mysteriously conceived child cast upon the waves of fortune because of a tyrant seems archetypal, however, and may be traced in numerous mythologies; the subject of such stories is not always holy or even good, however, and Mordred is not alone in this regard. The theme of the evil survivor is developed in a similar medieval convention concerning the infant Judas, with whom Mordred shares some obvious similarities. Malory may be unique, however, in sacrificing the innocents while preserving the demon seed.

It is of some note that Mordred was born on May Day, a highly significant date in Celtic mythology generally which is closely related to *Calan Mai*, which is to say 'May Eve' in the Welsh tradition. This medieval convention was derived from the festival of ritual purification and new beginnings associated with the ancient Celtic Beltaine holiday.[27] It is of special interest, moreover, that Calan Mai is the very day of the magical abduction of Pryderi, the great Welsh hero, in the First Branch of the *Mabinogion*. Pryderi was also fostered in ignorance of his true identity of course, a parallel detail which emphasizes

Detail of an historiated initial 'O' from a manuscript, showing an image
of King Arthur setting infants adrift in a boat.

Mordred's derivation from common archetypes of the hero generally
and of Welsh heroes specifically, as well as underscoring, in the final
analysis of his portrayal by Malory, his unique position as the anti-
hero of the Arthurian tradition.

Mordred's villainy is made manifest in a number of episodes in
which he is at once a bloodthirsty murderer and a craven coward, such
as that in which he treacherously stabbed Lamorak, thus slaying his
mother's lover. Lamorak was not only outnumbered by Mordred and
his siblings, but his death blow was dealt from behind; moreover,
Mordred and his brothers hacked the dead body of their enemy as
it lay upon the ground. In a similar act of cowardice and treachery,
Malory assures us, Mordred and Agravain murdered Sir Dinadan in
the midst of the search for the Grail. Mordred and his crony were
avenging themselves upon Dinadan for an earlier humiliation, coupled

with the fact, *Le Morte Darthur* tells us, that Dinadan loved Lamorak, whom Mordred hated. Dinadan revered good and those who pursued it, while he reviled evil and those who revelled in it; he and Mordred were therefore natural antagonists.

It is, of course, in his undying enmity for Lancelot and Guinevere – the right hand of the father Mordred hated and the love of that father's life – that Mordred's true nature is most clearly developed and manifested in the course of *Le Morte Darthur*. It was Mordred who with Agravain assembled the dozen knights who attempted to ambush Lancelot as he lay with Guinevere, although they paid with their lives for this foolhardy venture, all, that is, but Mordred himself, who fled – wounded – like a coward, anxious to sow further discord by reporting this evil of the queen and her lover to King Arthur. It was also through the events which followed this malicious unveiling of the adultery of Guinevere that Mordred's greatest plot was to unfold. After Lancelot returned to his own lands with the knights loyal to him, Arthur and Gawain followed him across the English Channel and laid waste to his territory as best they could; Mordred, meanwhile, as Arthur's own son, was left to rule the realm as regent, and to dispose of the queen as he saw fit.

Mordred's identity as a wilful minion of Satan is manifested not only in his sinful behaviour and hatred of those who do good and love Arthur, but in his overt dismissal and even contempt for the authority of the Church. This aspect of Mordred's nature becomes clear during his attempt to cuckold his own father: while Arthur was campaigning against the forces of Lancelot in France, Mordred forged letters from abroad declaring that the king had been slain and that Mordred, the rightful heir to the kingdom, should immediately succeed him. Arthur's faithless son then called a parliament, had himself crowned king and announced his intention to marry Guinevere, thus both cementing his claim to the throne should his father die and perfecting Arthur's humiliation should he return to Britain. The queen, meanwhile, although horrified and disgusted by Mordred's intentions, flattered him into believing her complicit with his lecherous and sinful designs; through enacting this ruse she managed to escape the clutches of her stepson and barricade herself within the Tower of London.

Enraged by her deception, Mordred attempted to recapture Guinevere by force. He was unable to successfully storm the tower, however, and so the queen remained safe, for the moment, from his grasp. The Bishop of Canterbury interceded at this point, rebuking Mordred for his licentious desire, reminding him of the irredeemably incestuous nature of marrying the wife of his own father (and uncle!), and threatening him with excommunication if he should fail to cease from his corrupt intentions. Moreover, the bishop declared that Mordred was a traitor who had falsely contrived to be king while his father yet lived. Not at all deterred from his course of action, Mordred was instead infuriated with the bishop, whom he both defied to excommunicate him and threatened with decapitation. The Bishop of Canterbury then acted upon his threat and cast Mordred out into the dark of damnation with book, bell and candle; that holy man then fled to Glastonbury, where he lived in the style of a poor hermit, and thus attempted to avoid the vengeance of Mordred, who, far from chastened from his excommunication, embraced his role as devil incarnate, continuing to conspire against and plot the death of his father, to lust after and to pursue his stepmother, and to hunt and attempt to murder the holy bishop who had attempted to correct his sinfulness.

When Arthur heard of the evil that Mordred had enacted and attempted in his unlawful assumption of the crown and sinful endeavour to claim the queen, he gave up his campaign abroad and returned forthwith to Britain. Mordred's army met his father's forces as Arthur came ashore, and with the bastard usurper was many a man to whom Arthur had shown favour; and so the most kind and chivalrous King of England was vilely slandered by those very subjects who had benefitted from his rule, fickle fools who cast their lot with Mordred, whose reign they called peaceful and prosperous. But ever are the men of England so fickle in their loyalties.

King Arthur threw back the forces of Mordred at Dover as the army of the true king battled its way ashore; but many men were slaughtered there, and Gawain himself received his death blow, and wrote with dying hand for Lancelot to return to his king. The knights of Arthur scattered the forces of Mordred again upon the Barham Downs, and the usurper fled to Canterbury. Messengers passed between the two combatants, and a day and place was fixed for the

re diff li contes he
qnt li rois artus se
tournoir acamaa
loth apres la mort
gaheriet uisca lassamblee · au
iour q lassamblee fu nomee pe

A miniature of Mordred accusing the queen of treason, as she
sits at a table with Arthur; early 14th-century manuscript.

two armies to meet: the matter was to be settled upon the downs
near to Salisbury on the Monday after Trinity Sunday.

## Arthur's anti-vision: an inversion of Constantine's dream

The night before that tryst was to be held, however, Arthur was gifted
with a wondrous and fearful vision in the depths of his slumber in the
midst of the night. It seemed to the king that he sat in state, bedecked
with gold, upon a throne mounted on a platform atop a wheel high
above a dark mere full of the most noisome and slithering monsters;
horrible worms and slimy serpents and foul beasts disported in that

dark and fearsome lake. Suddenly, however, Arthur felt the wheel begin to shift, and he quickly descended from the heights of his vantage point at the apex of the wheel's circuit. Down, down he swung, gathering speed, until he was cast headlong from his seat into the black waters writhing with disgusting creatures, which began to rend him limb from limb. Crying out with terror at this horrible fate, Arthur awoke from his dream.

After his horrible nightmare Arthur slept fitfully, neither falling deeply asleep nor remaining fully awake. Finally, as daybreak neared,

A *bas-de-page* miniature of King Arthur and his knights being attacked in their beds.

the king once more was granted a vision, although this one was more joyful to him. It seemed to him that he saw Gawain approach him, and that good knight was surrounded by lovely ladies. Delighted to see his nephew once again, the king proclaimed his surprise and joy, and asked the slain knight how he might thus miraculously appear, who the beautiful ladies were that accompanied him and what such a wonder might signify. Gawain replied that his companions were all of those ladies for whom he had battled in righteous defence during his lifetime; through the intercession granted because of their prayers, moreover, Gawain had been granted leave by the Almighty to appear unto Arthur and to warn him of his own impending doom. Furthermore, through the grace of Jesus Christ Gawain was empowered to warn Arthur that, although he was fated to die in battle against Mordred the next day – and many a man on either side along with him – Arthur might escape this destiny if he but compacted a treaty with Mordred for the space of a month and a day. If he were to enter into such an agreement with Mordred, Gawain continued, he would not only survive but thrive, in that Lancelot would land on British soil within that period in order to support him. If, however, Arthur battled his son on the morrow, then the king would surely die.

Arthur's vision of the turning wheel which brought him to the pinnacle of height in golden robes and upon a high throne only to cast him into the depths of watery torment, destruction and death is a clear evocation of the common medieval trope of the Wheel of Fortune, a theme which is closely related to and sometimes described in combination with Dame Fortuna or Lady Fortune, seemingly evoked to this day in the common allusion to 'Lady Luck'. A personification of fate who embodies the fickle and volatile nature of all the alluring rewards of this world – wealth, high station, honour, even health and life itself – any or all of which may desert one at a moment's notice without warning. The Wheel of Fortune itself serves to emphasize that earthly power and glory such as Arthur's are fleeting at best, and medieval pictorial depictions of such wheels, sometimes spun at the hand of Dame Fortuna herself, often portray a king crowned in glory on a throne at the apex of the circuit. At the bottom of the wheel one sees another figure, crown tumbling into the filth below, who is thrown from just such a seat: as one monarch rises, another one falls, and the lesson for Arthur – and for all who see such an image – is that only fools trust in the things of this world, however lovely or appealing. Arthur's nightmare is also an obvious reference to the dream vision, a highly popular genre of medieval literature perhaps best known through the vision of the Roman emperor Constantine the Great, who is said to have dreamt of a great cross in the sky on the eve of battle and to have heard a celestial voice announce, 'By this sign thou shalt conquer.' Arthur's dream was more dismal but would prove just as insightful.

## The final battle: Arthur and Mordred in mortal combat

When he awoke, the king summoned his lords and clerics to him, declared the import of his vision and demanded that such an armistice be reached with Mordred for one month and one day. Arthur's envoys then met with their enemies, and they came to an agreement. Although the terms of treaty were forged, however, the two leaders were required to meet to compact it, and each took with him to the middle of the plain fourteen retainers, while the rest of their forces looked on. Through mutual distrust, unfortunately, each leader had taken the precaution to warn his followers to attack without question if they were to see a sword drawn. Arthur and Mordred met as per their agreement, and the treaty was properly compacted; then wine was brought and they drank together. As they did so, however, an adder crawled out of the underbrush and stung a knight upon his heel. Reacting to the bite of the adder, the knight drew his sword to slay serpent, and seeing in this simple act of self-defence the treachery each side had feared of the other, each army sounded the attack and rushed headlong into the other.

All day the armies battled, and the slaughter was unimaginable: a hundred thousand men lay dead by dusk. Finally, Arthur spied Mordred, all alone and exhausted and sorrowful, and declared his intention to slay his son. Sir Lucan warned his king against this action, reminded him of the vision of Gawain and advised Arthur that, should he but let this one wicked day pass, all might be well, for Arthur held the field with two followers, Lucan and Bedivere, while Mordred alone survived of the rebel forces.

Miniature of the fatal fight between Arthur and Mordred,
from a late 15th-century manuscript from the north of France.

Nevertheless, unwilling to forego vengeance, whatever the cost, Arthur ignored the warning imparted through his vision of Gawain and charged Mordred headlong, impaling his son with his spear by plunging it beneath Mordred's shield and well into his body. Feeling his death upon him, however, Mordred forced himself down the length of his father's spear, lifted his sword overhead with both hands and brought the blade crashing down upon Arthur's skull, piercing it into the brain. Thus Mordred died, but not before dealing his father his mortal blow. Thus came to pass the prophecy of Merlin, who had long before foretold that Arthur would be met by his own son Mordred in a great battle near Salisbury.

Malory's critique of the vacillating loyalties of the men of Britain is thought by many to be a commentary on the shifting allegiances brought on by the Wars of the Roses; in a more mythic vein, of course, the disloyalty of the subjects of he whom Malory calls the greatest and most noble and just of British monarchs for a false, deceitful and tyrannical pretender obviously resonates with the foolishness of Adam, who ignored the commandment of his God, and of those who called for the Crucifixion of Christ shortly after welcoming him as a prophet. Although this association is not stated in so many words, Arthur's clear identification as a Christ figure, as well as Mordred's portrayal as a Judas-like betrayer and evil Satan figure, beg such an analogy. The adder seems particularly significant in this context, causing as it does the act which triggers the wicked slaughter on a day which otherwise might have proven peaceful. This passage seems to evoke the curse of the third chapter of Genesis, in which the snake is doomed to slither along on its belly, bruising the heels of the sons of Eve as they bruise

Miniature of the battle between King Arthur's and Mordred's armies on Salisbury Plain, from an early 14th-century manuscript from the north of France.

its skull. Moreover, given that the promise of life was snuffed out by the careless knight's action, one might well note the relationship between the resultant needless deaths of multitudes upon the battle-field and the great death provoked upon mankind by Original Sin, which was triggered by one thoughtless act of vanity prompted by the serpent in the Garden of Eden.

Mordred has a unique origin which indicates that he is unusual, but the sinful nature of his conception and the perverted purpose of the events which follow all serve to underscore this incestuous bastard's identity as an anti-hero, the ultimate villain who manifests and mag-nifies the worst qualities in his father's character. Indeed, Mordred's existence is framed by twinned attempts at familial murder, and it is perhaps most eloquently indicative of Mordred's incarnation of evil inherited from his father that Arthur's botched attempt at the infanti-cide of his son was matched by Mordred's successful attempt at parricide. In this light, Mordred's perverse desire to possess his father's wife sexually might well be seen to reflect Arthur's illicit union with Morgause. In Malory's telling, Mordred is developed into the verit-able antithesis to and eventual nemesis of his own father, whom he reflects like an evil mirror image.

## Christ meets Antichrist:
## Arthur and Mordred in cosmic conflict

It is of particular interest that Mordred reaches, in his treatment at the pen of Malory, his apex as a satanic anti-hero, the evil reflection of his own father. Indeed, the figure of Arthur, a Christ-like saviour born in the legends of the battles of the Britons for their very survival against the Anglo-Saxon invaders, is rendered most memorably as the king who is foretold to rise again after his battle with Mordred. The final battle between the forces of Arthur and Mordred thus becomes cast as a conflict between the armies of good and those of evil, and it is of particular note that Malory chooses to emphasize the damage wrought to the body politic through the dissension between British factions which should have stood shoulder to shoulder under the banner of the rightful king against external enemies. Indeed, the medieval mythology of holy war is generally cast in just such terms, and often illuminates just such concerns: although the armies of good should march in lockstep against those of evil under the banner of the one true God, too often, our sources inform us – with anger and chagrin – such cosmic battles are lost or even ignored altogether precisely because of petty squabbles, vanities and jealousies which divide those who should take arms together in sacred common cause.

Gustave Doré, 'Edyrn with His Lady and Dwarf Journey to Arthur's Court',
Plate III of *Idylls of the King*, 1867.

# 4

# The Once and Present King

M odern adaptations of Arthurian stories seem virtually endless, and in addition to literary works they include television series, feature films, cartoons, comic books, video games, board games and role-playing games. Some such manifestations wear medieval masks, some are shrouded in the Dark Ages which spawned the Arthur legend and some are modernizations. While it would be a quest worthy of the most fearless follower of Arthur to examine in detail every such work, the purpose of this chapter is to examine selected aspects of some of those modern-day manifestations of Arthuriana most significant to an exploration of their abiding appeal. Perhaps the earliest iconic modern-era adaptation of Arthurian mythology is Alfred, Lord Tennyson's *Idylls of the King*, dating in its finished form from the late nineteenth century. Not to be dismissed from the same period, would be Mark Twain's re-envisioning of this mythology through an American lens in *A Connecticut Yankee in King Arthur's Court*, which became a perennial favourite in its own right, and which has spawned its own set of film and animated descendants, ranging from a 1949 Hollywood release starring Bing Crosby through Disney's *A Kid in King Arthur's Court*, released in 1995. Novel adaptations of Arthurian narratives are legion, but a seminal version is T. H. White's *The Once and Future King* from the mid-twentieth century, followed by Mary Stewart's series of Arthurian novels, which explore in depth the figure of Merlin. *The Mists of Avalon* by Marion Zimmer Bradley, published in 1983, retold the Arthurian myths from a feminist per-spective, a particularly fertile approach for inviting comparative mythological analysis of Celtic goddesses manifested in Arthuriana.

*The Forever King* series by Molly Cochran and Warren Murphy brought a time-shifted Arthur and his court into the postmodern world, while on the opposite end of the spectrum, Bernard Cornwell penned a wildly popular series set in Dark Age Britain. Likewise, the film industry is responsible for a constant stream of movies based in whole or in part on the myths, folklore and legends of Arthur, often focusing on key archetypes which are perennially fascinating to audiences. Film adaptations range from Disney animation to the burlesque of Monty Python to the very recent Guy Ritchie production, *King Arthur: Legend of the Sword*, released in May of 2017. Notable television efforts include the BBC's recent *Merlin* and the Starz network's intense, if short-lived, *Game-of-Thrones*-style *Camelot* series.

## Arthur enters the age of industrial empire

It could be said that Arthur made his entrance into the modern era through the pen of Alfred, Lord Tennyson, whose *Idylls of the King* was in many ways a magnum opus to which he dedicated much of his attention over the latter decades of his life.[1] Tennyson's masterful Arthurian cycle, begun perhaps as early as his days at Cambridge, was notably spurred by the death of the author's friend A. H. Hallam in 1833. In response to this tragedy Tennyson composed his 'Morte d'Arthur', first read aloud to friends in 1835; the work eventually included a dozen separate poems touching upon the life, times and court of King Arthur.[2] The initial set of four poems was published in 1859. Tennyson's original 'Morte d'Arthur' was later folded into 'The Passing of Arthur', released with the second set of poems a decade later, and the remaining poems followed over the next few years. The final poem was written in the early 1870s but not published until 1885. Finally in 1891, the year before Tennyson's own death, the entire set was published in the form best known to modern readers. Tennyson's treatment of the Arthurian tradition shows intimacy with many of the major sources of Arthurian myth and legend available to him, including the works of Malory and Geoffrey of Monmouth, as well as the *Mabinogion*.

The *Idylls of the King* begins with the meeting of Arthur and Guinevere and ends with the mortally wounded Arthur's departure to Avalon. The love triangle of Arthur, his queen and Lancelot is an item of special focus, and many of the other tales seem to emphasize the virtues of their characters and relationships in ways designed to underscore the flaws of the primary trio. Adultery and disloyalty may be the sins which dashed the dreams of Camelot, but Tennyson's portrayal of courtly love and chivalric ideals both reflected and influenced Victorian notions of devotion and duty. In his position as poet laureate, and at the request of Queen Victoria, Tennyson dedicated his *Idylls of the King* to Prince Albert within months of the Prince Consort's death in December of 1861. This dedication both lamented the lost Albert as the most truly ideal Arthurian knight and indicated that Albert had been fond of the *Idylls*. Tennyson's dedication thus seems at one and the same time both sincere and savvy, since the association between Victoria's dearly departed husband and Tennyson's poems both offers condolence to the queen and guarantees very brisk sales to the author. 'To the Queen', a short poem appended to the collection, provides a fitting postscript that self-consciously draws a stark contrast between rumblings of dissent and discontent in Victoria's empire and the mighty storm of the final battle which destroyed the Arthurian dream. If British common sense should win out, Tennyson assures his monarch, such fears and unrest are phantoms of the early dawn, the shadows of which will recede in the brightness of the day. Thus the most familiar published version of Tennyson's Arthurian work is deliberately and self-consciously framed with overtly Victorian messages tying Albert to the Arthurian ideal and admonishing the British Empire not to fall victim to the internal dissension which ultimately overthrew the ideals of the Round Table.

In contrast to Tennyson's reverence for empire, one might expect a nation which twice cast off the shackles of British imperialism to offer a searing critique of quasi-religious reverence for a long-ago king; with a few notable exceptions, however, one might be flummoxed to discover that, if anything, Americans, even more than the British, seem to embrace the mythos and ethos of the Arthurian ideal. The one most notable exception, of course, is provided by our own Merlin of Missouri, Samuel Clemens. Mark Twain's Connecticut Yankee Hank Morgan provides an irreverent American perspective which lampoons the excesses of the dogmatic adherence to ritual and hierarchy of Arthur's knights, as well as the stylistic excesses of the genre of the Arthurian romance. Moreover, medievalism and Arthuriana were very popular in America – especially in the South – during Twain's time. These movements romanticized a world that never was, in order to valorize an idealized medieval age that provided a pretty – although utterly, laughably and tragically false – gloss on slavery. Indeed, Mark Twain laid the blame for the Civil War on Walter Scott.[3] The African American author Charles W. Chesnutt, among others, challenges this southern convention in a tournament sequence clearly evocative of Scott's *Ivanhoe* in *The House Behind the Cedars* (1900), which deals with black Americans passing as white in Reconstruction-era South.

Twain's work emphasizes that there is little to recommend the medieval world from the common man's perspective, obliquely criticizing the contemporary social structures associated with this romantic vision of halcyon days of yore. Along the way, Twain self-consciously and explicitly crafts a rejection of romantic, rose-coloured views of the past, a sort of 'anti-mythology', an inoculation as it were against the easy and comfortable adherence to archetypes of the great man, the noble cause and the 'good old days'. Although Twain's text and its approach remain popular, many contemporary adaptations thereof seem to have become vehicles for a sort of *Bildungsroman* of the protagonist, who in such works may be more concerned with self-development than social critique. Such latter-day Connecticut Yankees often seem markedly less sharp-eyed, sharp-tongued and sharp-witted than Yankee Hank Morgan, a protagonist ever ready to prove his own worth as a paragon of New World meritocracy as he gleefully upends a superstitious, intolerant and inept Old World aristocracy, even if his experiments fail utterly in the end.

Hank Morgan, the eponymous Connecticut Yankee, is a talented mechanic in the nineteenth century. Knocked out in a fight, he finds himself transported to the court of King Arthur in the year 528, where he is soon condemned to be burned at the stake. This offers Hank his first opportunity to illustrate his advantages as a man from the future, as he is able to accurately predict an eclipse, an act of apparent prognostication which allows him to save himself. Hank quickly rises in Arthur's favour and esteem, alienating the magician Merlin, who

Daniel Carter Beard, frontispiece from *A Connecticut Yankee in King Arthur's Court* by Samuel Clemens (Mark Twain), published in 1889.

becomes Hank's steadfast antagonist. Hank introduces all sorts of modern technologies and appliances to Arthur's realm, and even falls in love with the Lady Sandy and has a daughter, Hello-Central. Hank takes Arthur on an undercover journey through his land, showing the king the reality of the lives of his subjects, and attempts to do away with feudal and aristocratic structures in favour of democratic reforms, which raises powerful opposition. Eventually surrounded with his supporters in a cave, Hank is able to employ modern armaments and technologies to devastating effect upon his enemies, slaughtering tens of thousands with a mere handful of followers; after the battle, however, he is wounded while treating the injured. Merlin, in the guise of an old goodwife, offers to heal Hank, but in fact puts him in an enchanted sleep from which he does not arise until his own era. Awakening a man who now is not at home in the present any more than he was in the past, Hank is doomed to mourn his lost life and loves. Hank's sense of loss could be said to reflect that of Twain himself.

Published in 1889, roughly contemporaneous with the appearance in print of Tennyson's *Idylls* in the final sequence best known to modern readers, Twain's *Connecticut Yankee* offered something of a satirical American antithesis to the great Victorian Arthurian cycle.[4]

Moreover, although it would be going too far to call *Connecticut Yankee* a direct forerunner of steampunk, its engagement of time travel, its almost proto-science fiction literary sensibilities and, most especially, its anachronistic employment of industrial technologies from the Age of Steam, projected back through the centuries into the unsuspecting court of King Arthur, all subvert the expectations of the audience in ways which might seem familiar to steampunk aficionados. It is only fair to note that Twain was melding a variety of current popular traditions in his satire; there were, for example, a number of other time-travel novels roughly contemporaneous with *Connecticut Yankee*, most importantly Edward Bellamy's *Looking Backward*, published in 1888. In any case, Twain certainly poked fun at precisely the same sorts of medieval literary conventions and Arthurian social structures that Tennyson had embraced and revitalized for a Victorian audience, and which many Americans – and most notably Southerners – saw as an idealized reflection of their own class structures. Moreover, even Hank's fate, rendered unconscious through the centuries in a hidden cave, slyly both evokes a 'once and future boss' take on the 'Breton hope' and echoes Merlin's own fate of eternal imprisonment in a cave.

Twain's wry take on the Arthurian canon has proven both versatile and enduring, and has spawned an extremely popular Rodgers and Hart Broadway musical (1929) and a Bing Crosby film musical with a new script and score (1949), as well as a number of cinematic and television adaptations.[5] The musical versions, as one might expect, were primarily concerned with the protagonist's love affairs, and the trips to Camelot were framed like dream sequences, not unlike Dorothy's sojourn in Oz. Beyond its apparent working-class critique of stuffy aristocratic conventions and dusty Arthurian lore, *Connecticut Yankee* is perhaps indicatively American in that it offers an everyman protagonist who survives and even thrives in an alien and hostile environment by his wits and abilities alone. Like Twain's first attempt at a novel set at court, *The Prince and the Pauper*, published just a few years prior, this text invites the reader to see the commoner hero of the tale as a sort of believable alter ego, a workaday champion who enters the lists of court intrigue flying the colours of his reader. Moreover, the abuses inherent in the caste system of Camelot offer striking parallels to the race- and class-based oppression of the

American South and the wage-slavery of the industrial North in Hank's own time.

Most crucially, however, Twain is far too nuanced a critic of the human condition to imply that Hank Morgan has anything approaching all the answers. Indeed, the very fact that Hank becomes known as 'Sir Boss' emphasizes that he uses the power of technology and industry much as his antagonist Merlin uses magic, and underscores Hank's own dictatorial sense that his ability to create massive might somehow justifies his actions – however horrible – as right. This point is driven home in Twain's description of the aftermath of the Boss's final battle: Merlin's body, stretched out across the electrified wire, his face twisted in a death's head grimace, echoes all too clearly the carnage of the Civil War and presages all too vividly the horrors of the trench warfare yet to come. Twain questions starkly the efficacy of a war – any war – however just the cause, and however efficient the killing machinery. The reader, first swept along by Hank's charisma and adventures, slowly comes to an understanding that Sir Boss's unyielding sense of the primacy of his own ideas and ideals makes him in some ways every bit as totalitarian and despotic as any monarch. Hank becomes a 'temporal imperialist', as it were, impelled by a self-imposed 'modern man's burden' to better the lot of the natives, whether they want it or not. *Connecticut Yankee* is in some ways a scathing indictment of the arrogance of the industrialized world, and it is notable that many adaptations of this work include a far less rigid protagonist and a far less bleak conclusion than does Twain, who in the end offers at least as much a pointed critique of the self-satisfied, self-made Connecticut Yankee – and the nineteenth-century world which spawned him – as he does of the benighted sixth-century court of King Arthur.

### An Arthur for a brave new world: enter the once and future king

Much as Tennyson's vision of Arthur dominated the nineteenth century, T. H. White's *The Once and Future King* proved to be the twentieth century's most enduring and influential adaptation of the Arthurian tradition. Initially published as four separate novels, this work is both based upon and explicitly and self-consciously linked to *Le Morte Darthur* through the character of the young page Tom Malory, who – rather like *Hamlet's* Horatio – is instructed by King Arthur not to live and die for his sovereign by the sword, but to serve Arthur with his pen by recording the history and ideals of the court of Camelot. The four component novels of *The Once and Future King* are *The Sword in the Stone* (1938), *The Witch in the Wood* (1939), *The Ill-made Knight* (1940) and *The Candle in the Wind* (1958). *The Once and Future King* was published as a single volume in 1958, in which version the second volume was reconfigured *The Queen of Air and Darkness*. A fifth work entitled *The Book of Merlyn*, written in the 1940s but only published posthumously in 1977, provides what might be seen as a philosophical epilogue for *The Once and Future King*.

A key conceit of White's Arthurian universe is that Merlyn ages backwards, and therefore moves into the past with knowledge of the future, unlike Arthur (representing the rest of us), who stumbles into an unknown future, gaining wisdom mainly through mistakes and missteps.[6] Throughout the course of White's Arthurian Cycle, Arthur develops from the wide-eyed young page 'Wart' of *The Sword in the Stone*, the ward of Sir Ector and pupil of the bumbling Merlyn, to the young King of England who is beginning to think for himself in *The Queen of Air and Darkness*, to the loving husband and loyal friend who turns a blind eye to Guenever and Lancelot's affair in *The Ill-made Knight*, to the doomed hero caught up in the inexorable workings of fate in *The Candle in the Wind*. In archetypal terms, *The Sword in the Stone* is most concerned with the childhood deeds of the hero and his tutelage by a mystical shaman guide. *The Queen of Air and Darkness* offers that hero's fatal if unwitting mistake, the incestuous conception of the son who will become his nemesis. *The Ill-made Knight* is concerned with the budding love triangle which threatens to overthrow everything the hero has created, while *The Candle in the Wind* recounts the divisions and apocalyptic destruction which ensue when this adultery is unmasked. The ray of hope which lightens the darkness at the end of *The Candle in the Wind* is the hero's realization that, although Camelot is in ruins, the dream lives on.[7]

*The Book of Merlyn* darkens this glimmer considerably, which may explain why it languished for two decades after the publication of the other novels in a single volume. Like the letter by Clarence Twain appended to the final battle of *Connecticut Yankee*, the bitter postscript offered by White in *The Book of Merlyn* candidly condemns the war-like nature of the human race. Merlyn is still teaching lessons, although far less hopeful ones than in *The Sword in the Stone*: where he once transformed the young Wart into the forms of animals in order to teach the boy lessons about kingship, Merlyn now shows the decrepit and dispirited old Arthur the natural superiority of the creatures he causes the king to embody. More melancholy in tone and pedantically didactic than the other four novels, *The Book of Merlyn* in some measure shifts the focus of the Arthurian saga from a mythic account of the heroic rise and tragic fall of an idealistic king to a cautionary tale concerning how our best selves are held hostage by our own innate savagery.

*The Sword in the Stone*, the volume of the set most clearly aimed at younger readers, has long been the most popular. Released in 1963, Walt Disney's animated adaptation of *The Sword in the Stone* has in the past half century become something of a cinematic classic in its own right. As might be expected of a Disney film, this animated version is notable for the addition of some musical numbers and some striking visual sequences, notably that of the young Arthur transformed into a fish, as well as that of the wizard's duel between Merlin and Madam Mim, who at first blush comes across in this production less as a power-ful villainess taken from the mould of a Morgan le Fay or a Nenive and more of a figure akin to a comic blend of the cannibalistic witch in *Hansel and Gretel* and Ursula the Sea Witch in *The Little Mermaid*. On the other hand, Mim's apparent desire to consume – rather than simply to destroy – Merlin in this scene, although clearly played for laughs, seems noteworthy, in that it perhaps hearkens back to a femme fatale figure such as Nenive, who wishes to possess and control all of Merlin's power before discarding him. Moreover, although the film follows White's basic structure as a sort of prequel to the main aspects of Malory's account of Arthur – sandwiched in between the hero's miraculous conception at Tintagel and his coming of age when he draws the sword from the stone – the Disney protagonist seems less engaging and his shaman guide more muddled than their counter-parts in the novel.[8] In addition, although the transformation of Wart into beast forms in the novel seems an integral part of his education as a future ruler, in the film we see less of a progression of this sort, and his experiences as a fish seem to teach him little more than 'rule by might is wrong', while his foray into the world of squirrels seems focused on a tween boy's misogynist disgust concerning an icky girl (squirrel) and her unwanted attention.

The very name of the film tells us what the climactic moment must be, and only the youngest and least informed viewers would be unaware of the eventual outcome. While the book overcomes this lack of suspense by focusing on the details of the hero's coming of age, as well as on the richness of the lives and pursuits of the secondary char-acters, the Disney film is flatter in this regard: Merlin is more bumbling, Ector is more blustering and Kay is a bit more of a bully. Further, although in such a context of flawed older characters we might expect a story of the eventual rise and recognition of the innate superiority of the protagonist, in the Disney version the young hero has little to recommend him other than an everyman sort of appeal. Indeed, the film's Wart is a very believable boy precisely in the way in which he resists self-examination and formal education, and there is little except for the eponymous climactic event to mark him as notable. Although one might be tempted to see in this lacklustre characterization a democratization of the Arthurian hero, it might well be fairer to assert that the Disney studio played to its own strengths in terms of musical and visual appeal at the expense of the development of Wart's character.

Alan Jay Lerner and Frederick Loewe's *Camelot* opened on 5 December 1960 at the Majestic Theatre on Broadway. Whereas Disney's *Sword in the Stone* focused on the young Wart's coming of age in order to captivate children, the musical *Camelot* employs the romance and intrigue of the Arthurian love triangle to tell a story that adults will find compelling. The show begins at the end and looks back, evoking the theme of memory so important to the work, a theme notably embodied by the figure of Merlyn. *Camelot* ran for nearly 900 performances, closing on 5 January 1963. Richard Burton starred as Arthur, Julie Andrews was Guinevere and Robert Goulet catapulted to fame as Lancelot. Perhaps most significantly, this show is forever enshrined in American mythology in that its initial

Broadway run closely coincided with the Kennedy administration, a circumstance which Jackie Kennedy explicitly tied to the Camelot myth within weeks of the death of John F. Kennedy.[9] In an interview with *Life* magazine shortly after his assassination, the president's widow remarked on JFK's fondness for the play, and most especially for its wistful closing lines about the bright, beautiful moment in the sun that was Camelot; Jackie evoked this lyric to assert the legacy of her own husband's administration, which, though fleeting, would stand the test of time and be remembered as a latter-day Camelot. In this self-fulfilling prophecy, Jackie Kennedy conjured the magic of memory in a way that reflects both the nostalgia permeating the Broadway musical and T. H. White's vision of Merlyn, the keeper of the flame of memory as he passes backwards through time. A film version of *Camelot* followed in 1967, and there have been numerous revivals, national tours and even a 1982 HBO telecast of the production. White's emphasis on the importance of Merlyn has been continued and extended in a number of later works.

## Modern Merlins

As White's treatment of him makes clear, Arthur's wizened wizard advisor is a key figure in the Arthurian tradition, a character which has played a number of important roles over the centuries. Moreover, in his capacity as the manifestation of memory, Merlyn performs a key thematic function in the universe of *The Once and Future King* and the various adaptations derived therefrom, renditions of the story of Arthur which have proven highly influential in their own right. Perhaps in some measure as a result, over the course of the past few decades Merlin himself has been the protagonist of a number of popular manifestations of the Arthurian tradition. Mary Stewart's 1970 novel *The Crystal Cave*, to cite one prominent example, relates the archetypal heroic coming of age of Myrddin Emrys – better known to us as Merlin – who was destined to become the shaman guide of the young King Arthur. In this telling Merlin is the bastard son of the Welsh princess Ninian, and the search for his father is one of the fundamental themes of this book, as is the hero's journey to the underworld, here represented by forays into the eponymous

Crystal Cave. Merlin's father turns out to be Aurelius Ambrosius (a Latin eponym for the Welsh *Emrys*, or 'Immortal/Divine'), the elder brother of Uther Pendragon and thus the uncle of Arthur himself, making Merlin Arthur's first cousin. Over the course of the book series, Merlin finds his own shaman guide, Galapas, as well as a loyal sidekick in the sturdy Cadal. Merlin also has his own adventures as he discovers who he is, what powers he has, how he can shape and control some cosmic forces, how he can aid Arthur in his development and quest, and that he is moving inexorably towards his own destiny.[10]

In this telling of the story of Merlin, Stewart weaves together epic and archetypal aspects of the hero's journey with a thoughtful and detailed treatment of the tensions in Dark Age Britain between the new theology of Christianity and the ancient myths of the Celts and Romans, even referencing the ancient Near Eastern figure of Mithras, who was important in Roman Britain. Thus the biography of Myrddin Emrys, like that of Arthur in many narratives, becomes both a compendium of ancient lore as well as a case study of heroic archetypes. *The Crystal Cave* is the first part of a series of novels following the life and adventures of Merlin, narrated to the reader through hindsight by the ancient Merlin, trapped in his cave. The subsequent novels in the series include *The Hollow Hills* (1973) and *The Last Enchantment* (1979); the fourth instalment, *The Wicked Day*, published in 1983, recounts the Arthurian saga through the lens of Mordred, and is worth examining in its own right.

If *The Crystal Cave* ends with the genesis of the great Arthurian hero himself, *The Hollow Hills* includes the search for and acquisition of that hero's totemic sword and his subsequent ascent to the throne. The third volume, *The Last Enchantment*, concerns the events leading to and culminating in the hero's death and apotheosis, a process mirrored by Merlin's own experiences within the crystal cave. In Stewart's version, Merlin is gifted with 'the sight', but only when granted visions by the universal deity he calls 'the God'. In a telling counterpoint to Bradley's feminist vision of Arthuriana in *The Mists of Avalon*, Merlin's supernatural vision is overtly linked to sexual abstinence, and the Merlin of Stewart's telling is most mystified when dealing with women, who remain forever somewhat obscure to him. His power of the sight aside, Merlin explains in his own pragmatic terms how many of the legends of him were founded more in his knowledge and capacity as an engineer than in his magic, and at times his recounting of the prosaic basis for such stories reads a bit like the voice of Hank Morgan in *Connecticut Yankee*, highlighting the tension between fact and fantasy in the development of the mythic and legendary basis of this vital character of the Arthurian canon.

A screen version of Stewart's work, broadcast as a six-episode BBC series in the early 1990s and starring George Winter in the lead role, was titled *Merlin of the Crystal Cave*.[11] A number of other film and television renditions of the life of Merlin – and Arthur's adventures from Merlin's perspective – have also followed this trend. Notable among these was a star-studded television miniseries from 1998 with Sam Neill in the title role, supported by Helena Bonham Carter, John Gielgud, Rutger Hauer, James Earl Jones, Miranda Richardson, Isabella Rossellini and Martin Short. In this telling, the magic of the old ways is being eclipsed by the new Christianity; Merlin at first adheres to the ancient faith until he falls in love, and conflict ensues. Sam Neill reprised his role a few years later in *Merlin's Apprentice*, in which the old sorcerer awakes after half a century to find Camelot in dire peril. The most notable recent manifestation of Merlin-mania, however, was the highly popular recent BBC *Merlin* series, which has engendered something of a cult following. Running from 2008 to 2012, these 65 episodes track the development of the young Merlin as he comes of age and embraces his destiny. Arriving at a Camelot where magic has been outlawed by King Uther, Merlin finds guidance from the court physician Gaius, who secretly trains him to control his innate capacity for sorcery. Merlin is also mentored by a captive talking dragon living deep beneath the castle, a creature brimming with oblique and allusive wisdom. Merlin becomes the young Prince Arthur's servant, and at first the two loathe each other, but as they come to terms with one another it becomes apparent that their fates are inextricably intertwined. This series is especially notable for its attention to the development of the title character, and although it takes great liberties with the source texts, it appears to do so in a way intended to foreground the relationship between the young sorcerer and his sovereign, who in this version are close contemporaries. In addition, as we watch an ancient Merlin trudge by Glastonbury

Completed in early 2016, this sculpture of the face of Merlin on the
rocks of the cove just outside the cave that bears the wizard's name
was carved by Cornish craftsman Peter Graham.

For long, long after the fall of Camelot – a latter-day traveller on a
modern highway, melancholy with the memory of his lost king's past
greatness – we are reminded yet again of this figure's recurring role
as a repository of myth and legend. Most recently, a 2015 feature film
entitled *Arthur and Merlin* takes us back to the traditional archetypes
of the hero and his shaman guide; in this case, the eponymous bold
young warrior and reclusive old sorcerer join forces to confront an
evil druid. The figure of Merlin offers insight into Avalon from a
viewpoint distinct from Arthur's, and so we are allowed glimpses of
the king as he appears to his closest advisor. Merlin is re-envisioned
again and again in ways that reflect the nature of a given Arthur.

## A New Age Dark Ages Arthur

Marion Zimmer Bradley's *The Mists of Avalon* (1982) is also concerned
with the tension between the old religion and the new upstart
Christianity, but this text re-envisions the Arthurian myths from a

feminist vantage point, utilizing the voices and perspectives of the major female figures both to critique the archetypal heroic coming of age narrative of Arthur and to reinterpret the nature and mythic function of the lives of these women themselves. A film version of *The Mists of Avalon* was broadcast as a TNT miniseries in 2001.[12] In this telling, the central conflict is not just among the characters but between the great spiritual and religious forces arrayed in Britain during the time of Arthur: belief and worship of the Great Mother and the traditional spiritual practices and religious rituals of the Celtic peoples and the Druids were first eroded, subsequently attacked and finally completely silenced and subsumed by Christianity.[13] Bradley's Viviane is the Lady of the Lake, here a priestess of the old religion; her evil sister Morgause acts as Viviane's antithesis. Igraine is the sister of Viviane and mother to both Arthur and Morgaine. Morgaine and Gwenhwyfar – Arthur's sister/lover and his wife/ queen – represent the opposite sides of this conflict between the old and new religions. Bradley fleshes out opposing world views which literally as well as metaphorically shape the worlds they touch and dominate. Indeed, in *The Mists of Avalon* the borders between the worlds of faery and man are permeable but may shift and even close as a result of what people believe. Although Arthur is at first conceived as a bridge between these two worlds, Gwenhwyfar's staunch Christianity tips the balance in favour of the new religion, and Morgaine turns on her brother when she sees him as a traitor to the ancient faith which spawned him and which he was supposed to save. In order to inform her work, Bradley immersed herself in academic research of traditional Iron Age British worship of the goddess as well as active consultation with New Age practitioners of latter-day reconstituted rites and beliefs. *The Mists of Avalon* thus reinterprets the mythology of the ancient Celts in order to frame the conflict of the novel. It also draws upon contemporary visions and versions of Goddess worship in ways that help us to extend in new and valuable directions our understanding of the abiding appeal of the mythology of Avalon.

In a similar fashion, a set of novels seeking to set the Arthurian tradition within its historical context is Bernard Cornwell's *The Warlord Chronicles*, comprised of *The Winter King* (1995), *Enemy of God* (1996) and *Excalibur* (1997). Cornwell's Arthur is a British warlord, as in the early accounts, battling both internal strife and the external threat of the Saxon invaders.[14] The story is told retrospectively by Derfel Cadarn, once a warrior who fought at Arthur's side and now a monk recounting Arthur's exploits for Queen Igraine of Powys (not to be confused with Arthur's mother, Igraine of Gwynedd). In this telling, Arthur is the bastard son of Uther Pendragon, King of Dumnonia and High King of Britain. Mordred, Uther's grandson and legitimate heir, at the start of Derfel's story has ascended the throne while still a child, and Arthur is guardian of his nephew the king. Although in Derfel's account of events Arthur is betrothed to Princess Ceinwyn of Powys, he is captivated by Guinevere, Princess of Henis Wyren, to the usual disastrous end. Merlin in this version of the Arthur saga is a druid, and tension between the old and new religions is also an aspect of the tale. Unlike in *The Mists of Avalon*, however, this Guinevere is a strong proponent of the old faith. Galahad is a great warrior but no Grail knight in this telling, and Lancelot is his half-brother, an opportunist whose accolades are more to be credited to poems of bards than to prowess in battle. The first novel sets the scene of internal strife; the second includes Lancelot's bid for power, Arthur's betrayal by Guinevere and Merlin's search for the Cauldron of Clyddno Eiddyn, an overtly pagan Grail quest clearly developed out of the Welsh theme of the Cauldron of Plenty. In the final novel, Arthur is able to quell Lancelot and to defeat the Saxons at Mount Badon, with the help of Derfel and Guinevere. Arthur defeats Mordred – who has become tyrannical – at Camlan, and he commands Derfel to cast away Excalibur to keep it from the evil Nimue. Arthur then departs the scene on board the vessel Pridwen, never to be seen again in this world. As of this writing, a television adaptation of Cornwell's Arthurian cycle is said to be in production.[15]

Jerry Bruckheimer's *King Arthur*, released in 2004, was also an attempt to place Arthur within an appropriate historical setting. In the words of the film's publicists, this movie portrays the 'true story' of Arthur, and at least in its Dark Age setting, with Arthur as a former Roman commander fighting back the burgeoning Saxon onslaught, the film succeeds in fulfilling this laudable goal. The backdrop of turbulent times in a provincial backwater during a time of bloody upheaval is well conceived, even if the rest of the film exaggerates its stated historical accuracy.[16] Clive Owen stars as the Arthur figure, a Romano-British commander of Sarmatian cavalry, auxiliaries under obligation to serve a given term fighting for Rome. At the end of this term Arthur and his men, who have been fighting the Picts, join forces with the native Britons – including Keira Knightley as a woad-dabbed Amazon version of Guinevere, far more a descendant of Boudica than any medieval damsel in distress – to face the brutal Saxon hordes led by a somewhat laconic Stellan Skarsgård. Owen's Arthur seems to have been based in some measure on Lucius Artorius Castus, an actual Roman figure who may have served in Britain; the Sarmatians, on the other hand, were in fact an Iranian people who spoke a Scythian language and were renowned horsemen. The evidence supporting the idea that Lucius Artorius Castus was Arthur is slim, aside from the similarity in names, while the evidence that this figure was a commander of Sarmatian horsemen serving as Roman auxiliaries in Britain is slimmer yet. It is only fair to note that there are those who adhere to both theories, however, and thus the Bruckheimer film would not be totally without grounds to claim it is based on the reasoned supposition of a few scholars. To claim to be based on fact, however, is undoubtedly an overreach, albeit perhaps a forgivable one, given the general run of Hollywood fact-checking. More interesting to this study is that fact that the Sarmatians, who moved from Central Asia into the Urals region and thence into historical conflicts with other powers in Western Europe, have been associated by a number of scholars with the Nart sagas, the epic tales of the Caucasus region that some Arthurian scholars claim show striking resonance with elements of Arthurian myths and legends. Again, the evidence for such an assertion is much more evocative and suggestive than clear and definitive, but in a discussion of Arthurian mythology it is worthy of mention.

## Arthurian adultery on the silver screen: star-crossed lovers in cinematic Avalons

Earlier cinematic adaptations of the Arthur cycle have generally been less interested in historical context, although sometimes setting has played a crucial role in such productions. For example, filmed largely on location – including at Tintagel – and based at least in its broad strokes upon the work of Malory, the 1953 film *Knights of the Round Table* ushered in the modern age of Hollywood adaptations of the Arthurian saga. Directed by Richard Thorpe and starring Mel Ferrer as Arthur, with Ava Gardner and Robert Taylor in the roles of star-crossed lovers Guinevere and Lancelot, this lavish MGM production may be more notable for its production values than its take on the intrigues in the court of Arthur. Filmed using the most advanced techniques of its time, this film employed familiar tropes of the Arthurian storyline, most notably the tensions of forbidden love, betrayal and revenge. The result has often been criticized as more concerned with the spectacle of the process than with its content. Most of the major Arthurian characters appear, and many key sequences are appropriated from Malory, although never slavishly and never in ways which would undermine the Hollywood penchant for a good love triangle.[17] Still, this film was popular and turned a profit, which in Hollywood terms deems it a success. The film is memorable for its lush score as well as stunning visuals for the time, and was moderately successful critically, garnering Oscar nominations in line with its emphasis on form over substance.

The great Arthurian love triangle again took centre stage in 1963 in *The Sword of Lancelot*, originally released in Britain as *Lancelot and Guinevere*. Directed and co-written by Cornel Wilde, who also stars as the romantic lead, this film featured Jean Wallace as Guinevere and Brian Aherne as Arthur. In this version, Lancelot falls deeply in love with Guinevere while bringing her from her father's court to Camelot for her wedding with Arthur. Mordred plays a key role in this film: he is the evil antagonist who (as may be expected) brings to light the queen's infidelity and attempts to send her to the pyre. Guinevere is rescued by her lover, but only to live out her life in a convent, while Lancelot goes abroad to France. Mordred has a broader range than usual in this film, however, and slays Arthur, a vile act which triggers the climactic sequence in which Lancelot heroically returns from exile in France to set things right. Lancelot and Guinevere are reunited briefly on the eve of her final vows at the convent, and her piety causes Lancelot to look to his own soul and to seek atonement for his sins. The variations from the sources apparent in this film seem designed to foreground Lancelot as the hero and romantic lead, and ultimately to define his relationship with Guinevere in the terms of

Detail of a miniature of Arthur and Guinevere at a banquet;
Lancelot kneels before them, requesting permission to leave
the court (a musician plays the rebec in the margin).

a spiritual journey, the successful conclusion of which is his sincere repentance for his sins.

Perhaps more importantly, this adaptation attempts to validate the adulterous relationship between the lovers by introducing a significant age difference between Arthur and his queen, which provides subtle undertones of a generational conflict.[18] Arthur, in this telling, is by this point not a warrior who wins a kingdom or love through force of arms, but a king who commands the fealty of his subjects and the affection of his bride by virtue of his status alone. Lancelot, in fact, stands in for the king as his designated champion, and wins both Guinevere and her father's kingdom for Arthur through his own martial prowess. Arthur is thus by this point no young reformer or nascent hero out to make a difference or to establish his reputation, but rather the very seat of authority at the beating heart of any social problems. Within a medieval context a young bride would be no anomaly, of course, but the concomitant tensions within such a union were well known and widely criticized even during the Middle Ages, as any student of Chaucer's *Miller's Tale* – to cite perhaps the best-known and most crudely hilarious example – could attest. Guinevere's only path to escape the life ordained for her is the convent, the walls of which offer sanctuary and imprisonment in equal measure. Lancelot, on the other hand, who served as Arthur's right hand – first in gaining for the king his wife and part of his kingdom, and then by avenging the king's death and reasserting order and peace – has travelled the road from youth to established hero. At the film's end he looks back on his great deeds much as Arthur himself did at the movie's opening, leaving the viewer with a melancholy perception of Camelot without the bright flashes one might expect. Thus this film is perhaps notable in mythic terms in its implicit interrogation of the end result of the hero's journey, as well as in its exploration of the tensions inherent in the interrelationships among the old hero, his young wife and the young hero who acts as a surrogate or proxy for his lord in both sanctioned and unsanctioned ways, wielding the sword for the king, as it were, both on the battlefield and in the boudoir. In this context, the American title seems particularly apt.

The theme of May–December tension in the royal marriage was reprised in the star-studded but ultimately forgettable *First Knight*

(1995), starring Sean Connery, Richard Gere and Julia Ormond, which is also notable for its appropriation of the ancient abduction trope – with its ur-type derived from mythic Welsh sources – which in this case involves the villainous Malagant, played by Ben Cross. An interesting additional aspect of this film, which is developed directly from the American Horatio Alger myth, is Lancelot's rags-to-riches backstory, in which by dint of innate courage, ability and noble nature, a lowly itinerant swordsman rises to be the most celebrated knight of the Round Table (a fact lamented by at least one aristocratic voice at court).[19] Moreover, this New World trope is further burnished with a fairy-tale Hollywood ending, in which the old king sanctions the love between Lancelot and Guinevere with his dying wish, validating in one breath their true love and Lancelot's place as 'first knight' of the realm, while simultaneously underscoring his affection and respect for both the woman he loves and the young hero who has supplanted him in his wife's heart and at the Round Table. Whether intended or not, the Freudian overtones are even more clear in this film than in *The Sword of Lancelot*: at the end this Americanized spin on the Lancelot and Guinevere story relegates Arthur to an ersatz father figure who has come to grips with the reality – à la *Father of the Bride* – that Mr Right eventually had to come along and sweep his little girl off her feet. In short, *First Knight* seems to have much more to do with American than with Arthurian mythology.[20]

### Trying to get a head: *Sir Gawain* and the *Green Knight* on the screen

*Sir Gawain and the Green Knight* – a poem concerned with fertility, the cycles of the natural world and emblematic colour cues, as well as with evocative echoes of ancient ritual decapitations and their literary counterparts masked as beheading games – is in many ways the perfect text for discussing the deep mythological roots of the Arthurian tradition. It has seemed, unfortunately, extremely difficult to capture on film, where it has often come across as more laden with campy flashback than with mystical insight. Director Stephen Weeks produced two big-screen versions of *Gawain* about a decade apart. The first, *Gawain and the Green Knight* (1973), starred as Gawain the aptly named Murray Head, famous for the Judas lyrics on the original *Jesus Christ Superstar* album as well as for his 1980s hit 'One Night in Bangkok'. Nigel Green co-starred as the verdant knight in another example of fortuitously named actors. This version interpolated episodes from *The Knight of the Fountain* into the *Gawain* story in order to help to emphasize the connections between the cycles of the natural world and the hero's quest for knowledge and personal growth.[21] Weeks returned to the same material in *Sword of the Valiant: The Legend of Sir Gawain and the Green Knight* (1984), this time with Miles O'Keeffe as Gawain and the incomparable Sean Connery as the Green Knight, and added a context of complex riddles to Sir Gawain's journey of self-discovery. In both of these big-screen versions, the Green Knight is explicitly associated with the forces of nature he represents, and both films conclude with this fertility figure re-entering the soil from which he sprang. Thus both of Weeks's attempts to capture the poem on film – although seriously flawed – reflect discernible traces of ancient British mythology. A 1991 BBC version of *Sir Gawain and the Green Knight* followed the original plotline more closely, and in 2002 an animated version was produced. In 2009 the poem was also the subject of a BBC documentary in which the poet Simon Armitage traversed Britain in the footsteps of Gawain, and a six-episode version of the medieval romance was produced for BBC School Radio in 2014.

## Arthurian Americana: Camelot on the American living room floor

As popular as literary and screen adaptations of Camelot are, it may come as a surprise to many readers that the most long-lived manifestation of Arthuriana in American homes resides neither on our bookshelves nor on our ubiquitous screens. In point of fact, in many ways, the most abiding, continuous Arthurian presence in the United States over the course of the last century has been the *Prince Valiant* comic series, which has run since 1937, remaining a cornerstone of the King Features Syndicate since its creation by legendary comic artist Hal Foster.[22] King Features has been a jewel in the crown of the publishing empire of William Randolph Hearst for a century, and for the past eighty years *Prince Valiant* has made a weekly appearance in countless American homes every Sunday in the 'funnies'. In at least one way, the eponymous star of the strip is a hero with a backstory which subtly mirrors a key attribute of Arthur himself. A scion of the ruling house of Thule who came of age in the fens of Britain, Val does not know at first that he is a prince at all. Moreover, Val is a paragon of knightly virtue, displays masterful skill at arms and combines the mighty brawn of a great warrior with the cunning brain of a wily general or king. In many ways a knight's knight, Val is also an explorer's explorer, and his many adventures have taken him to the northern expanses of Thule, across the ocean to the unknown Americas and throughout the European continent and beyond, into the courts of Romans, Byzantines and others, to far-flung and exotic locales, including China and Arabia. Although the creators of the strip have never been constrained by history, they have utilized historical sources where practical, and it seems no coincidence that Val's sphere of action in many ways reflects the breadth and depth of the Viking world of which his character is a fictional part.

The range of exciting adventures and nature of his knightly prowess make him an ideal member of Arthur's court, of course, which in some measure explains his abiding appeal; moreover, Val's absolute dedication to using his might only for right and his complete adherence to the quest to bring light to benighted corners of the world marks him as a true bastion of the Arthurian dream, a dream particularly beloved by Americans of the early twentieth century and mirrored in the United States on the eve of the Second World War by icons such as Superman. Beyond these heroic characteristics, however, Val is also appealing in his role as an everyman of sorts, a family man devoted to his wife Aleta, Queen of the Misty Isles, and to his adventurous children who keep him on his toes in a way that any American father would recognize; this, too, may speak to Val's lasting power in the Sunday comics. Although the strip is quite original and in some ways very American, Val's story is firmly rooted in a world which revolves around Arthur, grounded by Arthurian motifs, structures and notable figures such as Gawain, who is often Val's companion. In sum, the strip has an elaborate history of complex storylines totalling thousands of weekly episodes and is still published by hundreds of newspapers across the country. With its combination of action, intrigue, exotic locations and carefully crafted, intricately designed artwork, *Prince Valiant* clearly can make a claim to be among the most self-consciously artistic of syndicated comic strips. Indeed, even the former King of England Edward VIII is credited with noting the central importance of *Prince Valiant* to the world of English letters, but given his personal history, this polite exaggeration may be more indicative of a love of American popular culture and fairy-tale chivalry than the realities of either literature or the royal family. The *Prince Valiant* comic series has spawned a number of feature, cartoon and television offspring, notably feature films in 1954 and 1997.[23]

It is worth pausing to note that, in addition to comics, films, television shows and cartoons, the legends of the Round Table have also entered our homes through innumerable computer games, board games and role-playing games. A good example of how some of the mythic tension of Arthur's court can be replicated in a game may be found in Shadows of Camelot, produced by Days of Wonder Publishers in 2005.[24] Shadows of Camelot combines some elements of role-playing within a board game context in a way implicitly designed to evoke Mordred's role as a traitor in the midst of the Round Table. Shadows of Camelot is designed as a collaborative game, and so all the players work together to achieve quests and objectives much as the Knights of the Round Table would. In this sense, the players are competing against the game itself, rather as a party works together to complete a campaign in a world created by a Dungeon Master in Dungeons and Dragons and other role-playing games of that sort. The fly in the ointment in Shadows of Camelot – the snake in the grass, as it were – is the 'traitor', a player designated in secret to work against the joint success of the group, while on the surface, like Mordred himself, appearing to work for the common good.

## Contemporary quests for the Holy Grail

The Holy Grail continues to be one of the most popular elements of Arthurian mythology, an aspect which captivates modern readers and audiences alike. The Grail plays a considerable role in some of the most notable modernizations of the Arthurian tradition; *The Forever King* series by Molly Cochran and Warren Murphy, for example, focuses on a replicating Arthurian saga in which the once and future king has been reborn as the ten-year-old Arthur Blessing in contemporary America.[25] Arthur becomes aware of his real identity after coming across an old cup which proves to be none other than the Holy Grail. In *The Forever King*, published in 1992, Galahad and Merlin have also been reincarnated, and help Arthur in his struggle to protect the Grail against the forces of evil. In *The Broken Sword* (1997), ex-FBI agent Hal – the reborn Galahad – summons the Knights of the Round Table from a mystical form of suspended animation to protect Arthur in the guise of a motorcycle gang. *The Third Magic*, published in 2003, is concerned with the modern-day survival of Arthur and his knights and the role of Excalibur and the Grail in the modern world, as well as with the age-old love of Arthur and Guinevere.

Susan Cooper's *The Dark is Rising* sequence is an award-winning children's series set in the modern day that involves a Merlin figure and a Grail quest in the context of a number of well-chosen and deftly interwoven elements from British myth and legend.[26] In brief, the young protagonists of the series join forces with the immortal Old Ones to keep the forces of the Dark at bay. The first book in the series is *Over Sea, Under Stone*, which was published in 1965; *The Dark is Rising* followed in 1973, and was named a Newbery Honor Book in 1974, the year that *Greenwitch* was released; *The Grey King*, published in 1975, won the Newbery Medal for American children's literature in 1976; *The Silver on the Tree*, the final volume in the series, was published in 1977. *The Dark is Rising* volume was made into a movie entitled *The Seeker: The Dark is Rising* in 2007, but the film adaptation changed many of the details most relevant to this discussion, and the film was not well received, especially by Cooper's fans.

Perhaps the most fully developed and clearly articulated Grail quest in modern cinema is to be found in *Indiana Jones and the Last Crusade*. In classic Lucasfilm fashion, this 1989 movie overtly organizes the details of a twentieth-century Grail quest around archetypes of the hero's journey which seem drawn almost directly from the works of Joseph Campbell. An opening flashback to young Indiana Jones's days as a Boy Scout gives a believable and engaging backstory for a number of his attributes and idiosyncrasies, including his trademark hat, whip, facial scar and fear of snakes. Furthermore, there is an innocence in the young Indy – played by River Phoenix – that the audience is encouraged to see reflected in his older self's singular vision and stubborn insistence on a particular understanding of 'the right thing', notably his quasi-religious belief that certain artefacts belong in museums. Moreover, in addition to classic archetypes of comparative mythology – such as the childhood deeds of the hero, the hero's search for his father and the hero's journey to the underworld – *The Last Crusade* takes on a number of explicitly Arthurian trappings, notably various bits and pieces of Grail lore which provide context for Indy's quest.[27] Set on the eve of the Second World War, the third episode in the Indiana Jones franchise returns to its roots, as well as to the broad strokes of a plotline popularized in *Raiders of the Lost Ark*, by pitting its protagonist, played by Harrison Ford, in a race against time to seek and to find the Holy Grail before it can be snatched by the Nazis, who wish to harness its powers to further their own evil, power-hungry agenda of world domination. This is a theme distantly echoed as recently as 2017, in the production of the History Channel's *Knightfall*, a series dedicated to uncovering the secrets of the Knights Templar, a mysterious order charged with the protection of the Holy Grail and its mystical powers.[28] If there is anything Indy should have gleaned from his race to find the Ark, however, it may be that divine powers are their own best guardians, and that he need not have been overly concerned on that account: like Third Reich flunky archaeologist Dr René Belloq and the disintegrated Nazis in the first Indiana Jones film, Dr Elsa Schneider learns, much to her chagrin, that the Grail is not a trophy to burnish her reputation any more than it is a weapon for Hitler's arsenal. Her shallow understanding of the Grail quest ends with her literal as well as metaphorical plunge into the abyss, a fate Indy himself avoids by heeding the wise and loving words of his father, played by Sean Connery.

This theme of divine retribution for the unworthy seeker of the Grail – perhaps derived ultimately from the medieval concept of the Siege Perilous – has become a modern Arthurian trope in its own right. For example, in episode ten of season eight (first aired in January 2015) of the popular Canadian television series *Murdoch Mysteries*,

Dr Iris Bajjali (who first appeared in episode five, season five, 'Evil Eye of Egypt') is an Egyptian archaeologist who is struck by lightning when she claims the Grail as her own and denies the existence of God. The devout Murdoch, on the other hand, who declares that no one may own what is God's alone, is spared. The booby traps in the resting place of the Grail in this episode self-consciously evoke various favourite counterparts Indiana Jones had faced, and just in case anyone has missed the joke, Constable George Crabtree, Murdoch's stalwart companion – and part-time writer of historical novels – suggests an idea for a story with an archaeologist hero straight out of the Jones mould. Even the episode's title – 'Murdoch and the Temple of Death' – pays homage to the second film in the Indiana Jones franchise. Although the first and third of the films have been criticized because the actions of the protagonist don't seem to have much bearing on the outcome of the object of each quest, in the case of *The Last Crusade*, the point is made explicitly by the character Marcus Brody early in the film that the search for the Grail is an internal quest for communion with God, a journey of the soul which ends in the spiritual growth of the quester. In this film Indy initially seeks the Grail as part of his search for his father, and he finds and uses it only to heal his father's wounds, in a sly allusion to the legends of the Fisher King, an Arthurian trope fleshed out far more fully two years later in a film of that name.

In *The Fisher King*, released in 1991, Robin Williams stars as 'Parry', a conflated figure who on some level represents both the 'holy fool' Perceval/Parzival Grail knight – as his nom de lunacy seems to suggest – and the Fisher King himself, a figure in constant pain whose wounds can only be healed through the compassion of the successful quest of a selfless Grail knight. In this case the flawed character Jack, played by Jeff Bridges, is wounded by his own sin and guilt, seeking and finding redemption through the quest for the Grail which heals the Fisher King. Thus Jack acts as an imperfect Grail knight, a jaded sinner wounded by knowledge of his own callousness.[29] Parry self-identifies as a sort of madhouse knight of the streets, complete with comic found-object arms and armour which reflect the literary Perceval's homemade accoutrements. The iconic Red Knight appears in the film as both a clear reference to a demonic villain of Grail lore and as a thematic lynchpin which illustrates Parry's madness; at the same time it links the modern and heartless streets of New York City, which drove Parry crazy and Jack to an abyss of despair, with the mystical and transcendent world of Arthurian myth and legend which in the end redeems them both. To ensure that the uninitiated viewer understands most of this subtext, this transformation and its roots in the Grail legend are articulated explicitly by Parry to Jack in a moment of intimacy in the middle of a darkened Central Park: the holy fool may heal the Fisher King by answering simple human need with an act of reflexive, unselfconscious compassion. Jack's quest to save Parry requires that he push aside his self-centredness and cynicism and become a holy fool himself; this accomplished, both are miraculously healed in a whimsical fairy-tale ending.

While certainly no fairy tale, one of the best-known and most abidingly popular cinematic takes on the quest for the Holy Grail is itself nothing if not a study in whimsy. As effortlessly erudite in subtext as it is over-the-top slapstick on the surface, the 1975 film *Monty Python and the Holy Grail* mocks the pretensions of Arthurian scholarship as adroitly as it appropriates and lampoons the modes and conventions of the Arthurian texts themselves.[30] In classic Python style, the film is more episodic than linear, but this format is perfectly suited to a parody of Arthurian romances, which are often themselves far more concerned with disjointed moments of action and adventure than with the narrative continuity which knits one such episode to the next. Some of these moments, such as the battle with the Black Knight or the appearance of the three-headed giant, clearly are meant to evoke commonplaces of the medieval tradition. A number of specifically Arthurian archetypes are also explicitly evoked, including the precarious bridge crossing and the mystical boat voyage. Obvious anachronisms, on the other hand, such as the Holy Hand Grenade of Antioch – not to mention lovingly rendered lampoons, such as the clapping coconut-shells for horses and the Trojan rabbit – reassert forcefully the modern subtext and subversive nature of the Python Grail quest.

In addition, familiar Arthurian tropes, such as the purity of Galahad, are parodied by extravagantly overblown sequences, such as the one in which the Grail knight is led into 'almost certain

Drawing of King Arthur encountering a giant roasting a pig.

temptation' by the Grail-shaped beacon which the dastardly Zoot (we learn from her twin sister Dingo) has set alight over Castle Anthrax, home to several dozen young and nubile beauties. Recurring jokes about the blatant cowardice of 'brave' Sir Robin, on the other hand, serve to mock the myth of the courage of Arthur's knights, while Lancelot's attempt to rescue Prince Herbert from Swamp Castle parodies the heteronormative commonplace of the knight's rescue of a maiden imprisoned in a tower. The murder of the droning Arthurian scholar near the beginning of the film provides a modern-day frame for the entire narrative, and emphasizes that such pedagoguery is the real monster slain by Arthur and his men, a theme coyly evoked throughout the movie with such sophistic exchanges as the hilariously groundless evocation of medieval notions of learning in the discourse on the nature of witches, to cite a famous example, or that on the airspeed velocity of an unladen swallow. Although Arthur and his men do slay a representative of the beast of pedantry, they feel the long arm of the law at the last, as they are carted off to a modern prison at the comically abrupt end of their quest.

The intellectual elite are often thought to take great pride and pleasure in pointing out the feet of clay of popular icons, so it is perhaps no great surprise that the Arthurian tradition, one of the most fecund and abiding founts of literary works and popular media of all time, should have spawned perhaps the greatest mockumentary ever conceived. The smart and sassy British slapstick cynicism of *Monty Python and the Holy Grail* turns a razor-sharp wit upon what it satirizes as an Arthurian mythos founded upon obvious historical ignorance, farcical origin stories, ludicrous sepia-toned visions of halcyon days that never were and (last but hardly least!) the laughably ridiculous self-important pedantry of Arthurian scholarship. But Monty Python's take on Arthur remains keenly relevant and immensely popular precisely because it parodies deep devotion to the ideas and ideals associated with Arthurian myth and legend; it is funny – in part because piling dung while expostulating political theory is hysterical – in large measure because the viewers know so very well the exact tropes the film skewers so brilliantly. Conversance with these central tenets is a prerequisite of getting most of the jokes, and so even this most anti-canonical of Arthurian texts serves in some measure to underscore and to perpetuate the very texts and traditions it mocks.

*Spamalot*, the Broadway musical based upon *Monty Python and the Holy Grail*, was a clear popular and commercial success. Its initial run on Broadway opened on 17 March 2005, and the show played for nearly four years and over 1,500 performances.[31] The success of *Spamalot* seems to have been based largely on the cult-like following of the original film on which it was based. It is only fair to note, however, that the Broadway show takes its source material and to a certain measure reinvents it, but in a way which clearly references the Python *Holy Grail* canon, including, to cite one key crowd-pleaser, the fearsome killer rabbit sequence from the film. The show goes further, however, both evoking some of the most-beloved Python touchstones from other films, including such fan-faves as 'Always Look on the Bright Side of Life' from *Life of Brian*, as well as spoofing classic musical theatre conventions, as in *Spamalot*'s 'The Song that Goes Like This', which skewers the obligatory Broadway musical inspirational anthem in a brilliantly self-referential manner. In a way, then, *Spamalot* takes Monty Python's interrogation of the tropes of Arthurian myth and legend to another level, placing some key elements of Grail lore in a context of campy twentieth- and twenty-first-century pop culture that might cause an introspective audience to question the very subtext of the quasi-religious fervour associated with certain key cultural touchstones, including iconic objects and recurring rituals. But then again, as the Python boys would surely note, it might not.

### The cutting edge of destiny: Excalibur, the sword in the stone and contemporary visions of Arthur

Based on a 2005 best-selling young adult novel of the same name, the 2010 Disney Channel original movie *Avalon High* offers an updated pop-culture spin on the Arthurian canon.[32] This includes some clear attempts to employ the familiarity of the basic storyline to subvert audience expectations, especially in terms of gender roles, at least in the film version; indeed, while the novel more traditionally equates the male star quarterback character with Arthur, the film shifts the focus to a female protagonist, although the two figures appear in slightly altered forms in both versions. Set in the midst of the all-too-familiar politics and social anxieties common to high schools everywhere, both the film and the novel offer classic coming-of-age tropes overlaid on Arthurian archetypes and plot lines. Arthurian heroes, villains and even Merlin take twenty-first-century forms at Avalon High, but although the 'once and future' Arthur trope is essential to the storyline – and putting the decision to foreground a female hero to one side – the underlying message of the film is a classic Disney spin on the fundamental American mantra of individual exceptionalism, the foundational assumption that all one really needs to do to succeed is to believe strongly enough in oneself.

This contemporary context of identity and self-actualization offers a striking parallel to the spin on the sword in the stone trope reworked in episode thirteen, season four of the BBC *Merlin* series (aired in 2013). In this, although Arthur has always been recognized as the rightful heir to Uther, Arthur and Merlin are in exile and on the run, and Merlin arranges for his young lord to pull the sword from the stone so that Arthur may prove his worthiness to himself; he will thus accept his destiny and come to believe in his obligation and ability to recapture Camelot from Morgana and Helios. Notions of hidden identity, innate ability and the unknown hero's battle with the demon of self-doubt are also at the very heart of ABC's popular series *Once Upon a Time* (2011–2018), and thus it is no surprise that the producers of that franchise chose to include some Arthurian elements which help to foreground and engage these themes.

The initial episode of season five of this series (aired in 2015), in fact, begins decades in the past with the child version of the protagonist Emma Swan in a cinema in Minneapolis in 1989, viewing the sword in the stone sequence from the Disney classic of that name.[33] Merlin appears to the child Emma in the form of a cinema usher, warning her that, when the opportunity unfolds itself to her, under no circumstances should she remove the sword from the stone, no matter how great the need or how seemingly good the reason for doing so. In the *Once Upon a Time* universe, Excalibur is actually the sword in the stone. It was forged from the Holy Grail, has been broken into two parts and is immensely dangerous. It is powerful enough, in fact, that it may destroy all light magic or all dark magic, depending on the will of its user. Arthur is an ambivalent figure in this series, and Excalibur and the sword in the stone trope are representative of mighty, elemental magical forces.

The Starz network's *Camelot* (2011) provides its own rather macabre twist on the origin of Arthur's sword and the identity of the Lady in the Lake. Giving both the source and name of the object a believable backstory which seems the stuff of folk etymology, it might best be termed Merlin's magic of fire and ice.[34] In episode four of the initial (and, as of this writing, only) season of this series, Merlin seeks to have the great smith Caliburn fashion a powerful, nearly indestructible sword for Arthur. When the sword is finished, however, the bad blood and mistrust between the sorcerer and the smith rises to the level of conflict when Caliburn refuses to hand over the blade and announces his intention to keep the credit for his feat for himself and to hand over the sword personally to the king. Incensed, Merlin demands the sword, and in the ensuing altercation the smith seems destined to take the upper hand. As he moves threateningly towards Merlin, sword in hand, the wizard draws upon his powers to direct the fire of the forge at Caliburn so that the smith is engulfed and destroyed by a ball of flame. Coming upon the scene of her father's terrible demise, his daughter Excalibur takes the sword, disables Merlin briefly with a blow to the head and seeks to take a boat to the middle of the nearby lake to drown the blade forever, and with it Merlin's hopes.

However, using his powers to freeze the surface so that he might stride out to her over the very waters of the lake, Merlin again unwittingly dooms one who would deny him possession of the sword he seeks. As she attempts to flee the wizard and discard the sword, Excalibur loses balance and plunges headlong into the lake; although she thrusts the sword up through the ice, she is herself trapped beneath it and drowns. Merlin takes the sword to Arthur, giving it the name of the girl and telling Arthur a more fanciful story of the origin of his weapon and the nature of the 'Lady of the Lake'. Thus, this version concludes, although the great smith Caliburn and his lovely daughter Excalibur were both collateral damage in Merlin's pursuit of a mighty sword for Arthur, their names and her drowning reverberate through the tradition of King Arthur and his signature weapon. This cynical postmodern vision of the self-serving nature of myth-making interrogates Merlin's functions in this capacity throughout the Arthurian tradition.

In perhaps the best cinematic appropriation of the sword of Arthur, John Boorman's 1981 film *Excalibur* takes Arthur's sword as its title, and indeed the possession, destruction, reconstruction and regaining of this iconic item underscores a key mythic concept of the film, the explicitly stated philosophy that the king and the land are one: the fertility of the land, the peace of the nation and the health and well-being of its people are all dependent upon the moral nature of the king and his spiritual relationship to his realm. Although Boorman's film purports to be an adaptation of Malory, there is also obvious resonance between certain scenes in the movie and aspects of Tennyson's *Idylls of the King*, and there are numerous episodes and themes drawn from other Arthurian sources.[35] Perhaps most notably, the central notion of the king's intimate relationship with his land

and the political, social and even environmental balance which derives from that intimacy seems to hearken back to ancient Celtic beliefs, including especially the Sovranty theme, the notion that the realm is the bride and the king the groom, and that the right to rule is both established and maintained through the proper balance and attention to this mystical union.

While there were those at the time of its release who embraced the film as a hyper-masculine assertion of political and military domination by strong patriarchal heroes, the film actually seems to indicate that it is the role of the privileged elites to ensure peace and prosperity of all through just action for the common good, and that to do otherwise is to court disaster. The film combines a number of characters and themes, and even the eponymous sword of the king is not entirely safe from this practice. The conflation of Arthur with the Fisher King, however, which has often been criticized, serves to emphasize the point that – as Perceval, who in this film supplants Galahad, explicitly articulates – the health of the king is derived from the health of the land, and vice versa. This particular episode vitally underscores for the audience the central importance of the relationship between the king and his kingdom in this retelling of the stories of Arthur. It is also worth noting that Boorman stated numerous times to critics and reporters that his film sought mythic, not historical, truth, a perspective that makes this film especially noteworthy in the context of the present study. This mythological subtext is underscored by the sword Excalibur throughout the film, as it provides a consistent barometer concerning the king's relationship to his realm and his ability to rule: Excalibur marks Arthur out as the rightful king in the first place; the sword breaks when Arthur uses it for the sake of his own vanity; Merlin's capture and imprisonment results when Arthur uses Excalibur to signal his own heartbreak by plunging it into the soil by the sleeping Lancelot and Guinevere; Arthur's estranged wife returns the sword to him in his hour of need when they are reconciled and the heartbreak is healed; it is through the agency of Excalibur that Arthur wins his final victory; and Excalibur marks Arthur's apotheosis when Perceval casts it to the Lady of the Lake, and the once and future king sails off to Avalon.

## Arthur live! Appropriations of Avalon
## in contemporary performance

Arthur is alive and well in myriad live-action venues, as well. To cite one recent and illuminating example, the 2016 Pennsylvania Renaissance Faire Halloween Themed Weekends wove elements of Arthurian legend into a context of the 1509 court of King Henry VIII, recasting Henry as a 'once and future' Arthur destined to save his kingdom from the clutches of the evil Morgan le Fay.[36] Although the Pennsylvania Renaissance Faire traditionally sets its events during the reign of Elizabeth I, in recent years the earlier court of her father has become the backdrop for its activities and dramatic episodes. The court of Henry VIII, in fact, is an ideal venue for illustrating how the British monarchy appropriated the legends of Arthur for political and propagandistic ends.

A bit of history helps to explain why this appropriation was politically expedient: Henry VII came to the throne in 1485, effectively ending the chaotic period of the Wars of the Roses with the imposition of a strong Tudor monarchy. The Tudors self-consciously embraced the concept that through the person and family of Henry Tudor, England was once again made whole, a notion which neatly aligns with the 'Breton hope' of the 'once and future king', and which was symbolized graphically through the image of the Tudor Rose. This symbol was intended to indicate the union of the Red Rose of Lancaster and the White Rose of York, thus emblemizing the final end of the Wars of the Roses and the union of the two great warring houses through the persons of Lancastrian Henry VII and his wife Elizabeth of York – Edward IV's daughter – to whom Henry was married in 1486.

Arthurian romances, notably popularized by Chrétien de Troyes, continued to please audiences throughout the Middle Ages and into the early modern period; indeed, the printing in English of Malory's wildly popular *Le Morte Darthur* took place in 1485, and thus coincided with Henry Tudor's ascent to the throne. In addition, the Tudors actually claimed descent from Arthur, thus in effect submitting that Henry VII's rise to power was a return to the Arthurian dynasty. Henry VII's elder son was named Arthur explicitly to evoke such an

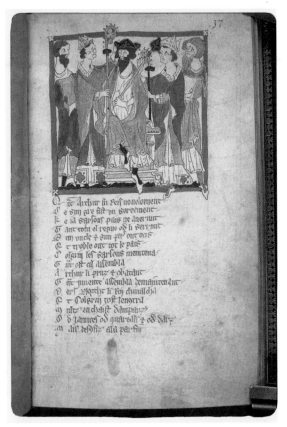

Drawing of the coronation of Arthur.

association, although as it happened Arthur Tudor died young and his brother Henry came to the throne. Henry VIII himself intentionally cultivated the Tudor association with King Arthur, commanding, for example, that the great Round Table at Winchester be repainted with Henry himself depicted as the once and future king, a great monarch in the mould of Arthur, stepping, as it were, from the pages of Malory.

All of this historical context provides an illuminating backstory which explains how the Arthurian symbols, figures and episodes appropriated by the Pennsylvania Renaissance Faire have some basis in Renaissance politics and propaganda, a fact which in turn indicates how the Tudors recognized the abiding appeal and power of the Arthurian canon five centuries ago. Moreover, clearly the producers of the Pennsylvania Renaissance Faire recognized and exploited the fact that the popular appeal of these legends and their connection to the British Crown has not much diminished, even if the political utility of such an association has faded.

In its 2016 Halloween Themed Weekend production, the Pennsylvania Renaissance Faire explicitly appropriated and employed three main Arthurian aspects: the person of Morgan le Fay, in this case depicted as the very embodiment of Evil in the form of a witch antagonist to the once and future king; the concept of the 'Breton hope', manifested as Henry VIII, who comes to the realization of his role as Arthur's heir literally on the very eve of his coronation; and the sword in the stone, here conflated with Arthur's personal weapon Excalibur, which magically eludes Morgan le Fay, marks Henry VIII as the once and future king and rightful ruler of all England, and provides Henry with the means to defeat and to destroy Morgan le Fay.

## Arthur on the open road: Avalon as a moveable feast

No discussion of Arthurian elements in contemporary Renaissance fairs would be complete without an examination of *Knightriders*, George A. Romero's 1981 exploration of the relationship and resonance between the utopian elements of the myths and legends of Arthur and late twentieth-century American countercultural ideals. Indeed, Romero's nuanced vision of the alternative culture manifested in such a sideshow – Camelot and carny in roughly equal measure – clarifies the fact that, however commodified the 'Ye Olde Renaissance Fayre' phenomenon may have become, it seems to have at its heart a kind of false nostalgia, a sublimated desire for a simpler, more idealistic age, one in which good and evil are ultimately identifiable, and one in which the struggle for the good is always laudable and worthwhile, even when doomed.[37] This perspective, however naive and flawed it may be thought to be, has always been vastly appealing in American society, the fact that such 'Goode Olde Dayes' – where not entirely fictive – were brutish and brief, notwithstanding. *Knightriders* follows the adventures and misadventures of a roving band of motorcycle jousters, a medieval fair of sorts, an itinerant troupe of misfits who have rejected mainstream American consumerism for the freedom to live as they please, paying their way through the hard currency of the blood, sweat and tears of their travelling roadshow.

In the film Billy, the 'King William' of the Knightriders, has attempted to develop a communal identity based on ideals in direct opposition to the common understanding of the American dream. The group enacts mock battles in armour on motorcycles, performing for gawking crowds who represent exactly the lives the Knightriders reject. Although Billy and some of his followers – including his own Merlin – believe in the spiritual purity of the quest their lives represent, others have been drawn into the Knightriders less out of a common cause than a common enemy: an America with no place and little tolerance for anyone who doesn't fit in because of race or sexuality or aspirations. Still others, such as Billy's main antagonist, Morgan, simply enjoy the opportunity to engage in mindless violence and be rewarded for a penchant and aptitude for mayhem. Billy is rigid in his understanding and articulation of the code of knightly virtues he embraces, however, and eventually the Knightriders are ripped apart by the tension between idealist and opportunists within the group, and the latter split off to cash in on their anachronistic lifestyle in a glitzy Vegas act. These black sheep eventually return to the fold when they are sickened and disheartened by the shallowness of selling out as a freak show on wheels, an existence that Billy had intended as a meaningful life built around devotion to notions of latter-day chivalry. The conflict within the group reaches its climax as Morgan's knights fight Billy's champions in a pitched battle royale to determine the future of the Knightriders. When Morgan's side wins, he replaces Billy as king, and Billy, philosophical, leaves to become a knight errant of sorts who seeks justice for the downtrodden and bequeaths his sword to his son before meeting his destiny on the open road.

*Knightriders* explicitly engages the concept that the Camelot sought by Billy and his true-believer followers is a community forged through a shared idyllic vision, a collective state of mind that rejects the prosaic and mundane elements which permeate rampant American consumerism. More than that, however, Billy emerges as a flawed but noble dreamer, a Grail knight who would understand all too well Marcus Brody's admonition to Indiana Jones that the search for the

Cup of Christ is a journey of self-exploration and divine communion. Leaving his fellow Knightriders in the care of their new king, Billy embarks on a final vision quest and – having done his best to forge a like-minded community, to right the wrongs in the world around him and to pass along his hard-won wisdom to the next generation – comes closest to spiritual purity as he flies down the road on the wings of a dream, right into the grill of an oncoming truck. Thus Billy is granted an apotheosis of sorts, having achieved as much of his ideal vision as the American highway seemed destined to yield.

## The children of Camelot: Arthurian tropes in blockbuster fantasy franchises

It is worth noting that some of the most enduring popular novel and film franchises of all time draw explicitly upon Arthurian tropes, in addition to manifesting common archetypes of comparative mythology. Although Harry Potter, for instance, shares in common with Arthur Pendragon mysterious origins, notable childhood deeds and the explicit identity of the 'chosen one', the same might be said for countless heroes throughout world literature. The fact that Harry Potter's mentor Professor Dumbledore bears more than passing similarity to Arthur's shaman guide Merlin, however, seems more self-conscious than coincidental.[38] Moreover, Harry's ability – as a true heir of Godric Gryffindor – to pull the Sword of Gryffindor from the Sorting Hat in a moment of dire need in the Chamber of Secrets seems designed to draw upon the traditions of both Excalibur and the sword in the stone. In addition, the fact that Harry's best friend Ron Weasley is later able to help Harry retrieve the same sword from the bottom of a pool of water evokes Excalibur's resting place with the Lady of the Lake. The most overt Arthurian symbol in the Harry Potter universe is the Goblet of Fire, the prize in a sort of competitive quest that turns out to be an evil inversion of the search for the Holy Grail, in that this object and the contest to win it have been subverted by the forces of the wicked Voldemort to lure, trap and destroy the 'chosen one' who stands in the way of the total dominion of dark powers.

In *The Lord of the Rings*, on the other hand, the re-forging of the broken shards of Isildur's sword Narsil into Andúril is clearly intended to mark Isildur's descendant Aragorn as the returning King of the West from which the last novel in the trilogy takes its name. If Aragorn corresponds to Arthur, moreover, Frodo Baggins plays the role of a Grail knight of sorts, set on a seemingly impossible, inverse quest to destroy the One Ring, a supernatural artefact that serves as an anti-Grail, as it were. In any case, the battle for Tolkien's Middle Earth – like that of the Narnia of his friend C. S. Lewis – is fundamentally the conflict between good and evil which is at the heart of the Grail quest.[39] Frodo also takes on something of the trappings of a type of Fisher King, maimed in the course of his quest with a wound from a Morgul-blade of such evil that it can never fully heal. That wound and the burden of carrying the Ring on the quest for its destruction so scar Frodo that, like Arthur, he takes an elven ship to Valinor, the otherworldly land of the fairies (here called elves) where he may finally be at rest. He is accompanied on much of his quest and even his final passage by Gandalf, a wizard clearly and – given J.R.R. Tolkien's stature as a pre-eminent medievalist – quite intentionally cut from the cloth of Merlin's robe.

As these many modern examples make clear, the tales of King Arthur and his court – and the aura of a Golden Age that surrounds them – pass from generation to generation and from nation to nation, transformed with each new telling to fit the expectations and needs of the audience at hand. This reality begs a final question, one with which we will wrestle in the conclusion that follows. Whoever Arthur was, may have been or once represented, who is Arthur to us and what does he mean today? In short, why does Arthur continue to abide?

# Conclusion:
# Why does Arthur Abide?

That Arthur, the 'once and future' King of Britain, would be perennially popular in Britain seems self-explanatory: the promise of a saviour who will arise in a nation's greatest hour of need is eminently desirable and not at all uncommon. After all, flowing under the details of the heroic life and tragic death of Arthur, King of the Britons, is a strong undercurrent of the Breton hope, the enduring notion that Arthur will return to reign once more. What is of greater interest is how widespread Arthur's reputation and popularity became and why Arthur continues to be revised and updated right up to the present day.

### Reflecting the face of Arthur in the mirror of desire

Rather like the Mirror of Erised in the world of Harry Potter, King Arthur is a darkened glass in which each succeeding generation can see reflected its desires, its dreams and its aspirations; each era has reinvented Arthur to suit its own contexts and ends. The Tudors, for example, exploited a supposed link to Arthur in an overt appeal to the abiding reflex of the Breton hope, for example, and thus could be construed as an anointment of sorts upon the House of Tudor, which promised to heal deep national wounds of disunity and civil strife. Tennyson evoked Arthur in a Victorian context as a call to arms concerning the needs and responsibility of empire, a position explicitly rebuked by his American counterpart Twain. White's vision of *The Once and Future King* offered glimpses of hope and light in the dark days of the Second World War and the Cold War which followed,

Tintagel Arch is part of the ruins of the 13th-century castle.
Richard, Earl of Cornwall (1209–1272), the only brother of Henry III,
may well have built the castle specifically to recall the stories of Arthur
and thereby to burnish his own status.

although this vision appears to have been darkened considerably in a jaundiced postscript that seems to hearken back to Twain's subtext of doubt of the efficacy of force and distrust of the motives of authority. More current visions of Arthur often seem to focus on contemporary myths surrounding notions of individual exceptionalism, although at their best they may provide aspirational figures which are dedicated to serving the greater good and which embrace the value of self-sacrifice. We in the twenty-first century are no different, and so it is no surprise that we have reinvented Arthur to suit contemporary tastes, to embody a postmodern sense of heroism and to confront current sensibilities of evil.

## Arthur as diamond in the rough: an unlikely lad as reluctant king

As of this writing, the most recent big-budget adaptation of Arthurian lore is Guy Ritchie's *King Arthur: Legend of the Sword*, released in 2017. This contains a great many legendary episodes, mythic archetypes and literary elements, some of them Arthurian, some not, all mixed together with a healthy dollop of graphic carnage, magic and mayhem into a witch's brew of modern popular culture, liberally seasoned with random bones of ancient traditions.[1] As the title suggests, the legendary sword Excalibur is an important aspect of the film, as is the sword in the stone trope, although the hero's rage-against-the-machine vibe and his misfit crew of ragtag heroes seems perhaps more appropriate to another popular folk hero, Robin of Locksley and the Merry Men of Sherwood, than to King Arthur and the Knights of the Round Table.

The plot can be hard to follow and sometimes seems subservient to the visual effects and nearly non-stop action, but in its broad strokes it involves Uther Pendragon defeating Mordred, who is something of a witch-king in this telling. Uther's brother Vortigern then utilizes dark magic and sacrifice to usurp the throne and slay his brother; the human sacrifices in the film, it is only fair to note, seem to hearken in some measure back to aspects of the early Arthurian canon. Uther's infant son eludes his uncle's clutches, drifting to safety in a manner reminiscent of Mordred's own infant escape, which of course itself draws upon the story of Moses in the bulrushes. Arthur comes of age surviving in the backstreets, a graduate of the school of hard knocks. Eventually he comes to the attention of Vortigern, who has been using the sword in the stone to try to identify his brother's rightful heir in a spin on an inverted, latter-day Slaughter of the Innocents scenario. Arthur is able to pull the sword from the stone, of course, escapes from custody and after a great deal of soul-searching embraces his identity, masters his mighty sword, defeats Vortigern and is crowned king. Along the way Arthur encounters battles great and small, mystical visions of both past and potential future, the Lady of the Lake and adventures and misadventures galore. The film ends at the dawn of Arthur's reign, with the implicit suggestion that *The Legend of the Sword* might soon be followed by *The Knights of the Round Table*.

Ritchie provides a backstory for his hero's mysterious origins designed as a clear inversion of the biblical account of the baby Moses: here the foundling is discovered and reared not by an Egyptian princess, but rather by a London prostitute; so while Moses was a slave raised as a prince in a palace, Arthur is a prince raised as a guttersnipe in a whorehouse. This setting permits this Arthur to be an underdog, a crucial element of much modern heroic ideology, without in any way undermining his ultimate identity as the 'punk who would be king'. This duality allows for the employment of yet another favourite modern myth, the rags-to-riches motif, concomitant in this saga with the inherent notion that Arthur's heredity is destiny and that, despite his self-doubt, he is fated to be king. This identity is emphasized by the sword in the stone scene and Arthur's subsequent confrontation with his evil uncle Vortigern in the dungeons.

Once Arthur has the sword, he must learn to control its overwhelming power at the same time that he must confront his own identity and destiny. Thus one might perhaps be tempted to look more to the young Luke Skywalker of the *Star Wars* franchise than the early Arthurian sources for a hero's journey closely parallel to this one, while the plenitude of magic and mages renders the story into a sort of *Harry Potter* versus *The Lord of the Rings*, with Mordred in flashback as some sort of amalgam of the archetypal Dark Lord. Though critically reviled, the film does embrace and emphasize a few key discernible Arthurian elements, and the battle scenes, in particular, have impressive elements; many critics have noted that the film's emphasis on graphic violence, special effects and action sequences in a dark and gritty medieval setting seems to have been influenced by the wide appeal of *Game of Thrones*, a suggestion buttressed by the appearance in the movie of a familiar face or so from the HBO series. In the end, however, *King Arthur: Legend of the Sword* embraces bright and positive aspects of the Arthurian saga, cutting off the story with the assembly of the Round Table, long before the dark and inevitable fall of all Arthur holds dear. This tells us a lot about the sensibilities of popular film-makers, of course, but it is also a fair barometer of what we in our culture yearn for in any story about any hero, and thus this film, however flawed, offers us an Arthur clearly scripted for our times.

## Arthur in the age of Westeros

In this sense, of course, *King Arthur: Legend of the Sword* lacks the killer instinct of a noir *Game of Thrones* cinematic sensibility. George R. R. Martin's novels and the HBO series based upon it overtly attempt to subvert the expectations of the archetypal hero's journey in general and of the Arthurian boy-destined-to-be-king in particular, generally killing off horribly those characters we allow ourselves to love or even to root for, and self-consciously turning on its head the common heroic paradigm. A caveat to the cynical, world-weary *Game of Thrones* aficionado is in order, however. Bad things happening to good people is not at all an alien concept in Avalon; on the contrary, it has always been a crucial component of Arthurian mythology and legend: Lancelot falls in love with Guinevere; Arthur has a son through incest; Mordred and Arthur fight to the death. Camelot by definition is fleeting, and its whole mystique is a veil of nostalgia for a lost golden age, whether or not said halcyon days of yore ever really existed. Martin didn't invent this trope, although he did foreground it, develop it into the signature archetype of his universe and – especially in the HBO version of his epic series of novels – slather it in blood and gratuitously graphic violence and sex. Further, it is crucial to remember that, although *Game of Thrones* is undoubtedly wildly popular, so were the *Lord of the Rings* and *Harry Potter* franchises, which notably leaven their necessary darkness with considerable brightness and hope, especially in their closing chapters. How *Game of Thrones* concludes, as yet an open question, will tell us whether and how far it embraces the flickering, faint hope that Arthur offers even at his darkest hour.[2] Finally, it is also noteworthy that while the Starz *Camelot* series attempted a *Game of Thrones*-style approach, it was short-lived, while the recent BBC *Merlin* series had a full run, and it tempered darkness with hope. In short, those who think that the common world view of the twenty-first century is darker and less hopeful than that of the Middle Ages which enshrined the myths of Arthur are betraying considerable ignorance of the realities of medieval life and death.

## The Arthur within: the quest for good

The fact that a warrior hero developed into a messianic figure, a dying god sacrificed for his people and ideals but destined to return, goes a long way towards explaining why Arthur and associated elements of his legend continue to flourish. As the core elements of a legendary Romanized Briton who stemmed the onslaught of a marauding invader – however briefly – became imbued with hagiographical elements from Christian saints' lives, Arthur became ever more associated with the Christian faith of his people, a nation at bay, a flock of God's sheep locked in a life-and-death struggle against wolfish pagan hordes clearly acting under the influence of Satan himself. As the later medieval Arthurian tradition developed, this opposition between good and evil remained, even though Arthur's struggles and enemies were no longer overtly pagan. Finally, the development of the great Arthurian Grail quest firmly fixed the notion of the members of the court of the Round Table as holy warriors devoted to seeking God's truth, justice and wisdom, even in the face of seemingly insurmountable odds. However ancient and pagan their origins might have been, in the High Middle Ages their battles and knightly virtues were all wrought into a means to the Christian God's ends, and thus Arthur's knights were recast into agents of no less than Providence itself.

Arthur – or perhaps it would be fairer to suggest that each of these manifestations is a distinct and different Arthur – changes to fit the needs of each particular context. Every place and age refashions

Unveiled in April of 2016, Rubin Eynon's 2.5-metre (8-ft) bronze scuplture *Gallos* (meaning 'power' in Cornish) is perched on a high point on Tintagel Island. The figure looks out over the key sites and digs on the island and across to the mainland of Cornwall.

Arthur to suit itself. It may be that the secularization of contemporary society has left a cultural vacuum which is often filled with super-heroes and other cultural manifestations of the forces of good, right and justice, ever at war with the evil all too obviously prevalent in a world that is clearly not fair.

Moreover, in a contemporary society which often eschews and at times even demonizes overt religious fervour, the trope of the once and future king offers a secular Christ figure, an icon of a saviour in times in which age-old belief in divine salvation has waned. Alterna-tively, among those who do embrace traditional religious beliefs, Arthurian motifs which manifest mythic archetypes may well align with foundational understandings of the cosmic struggle between good and evil as this plays out in the temporal world. Further, although such believers might well balk at the explicit application of a rubric of comparative mythology to their own faith tradition, the implicit resonance between the central icons of such traditions and their Arthurian counterparts might serve to make many key tales of Camelot palatable – perhaps even desirable – to such an audience, especially given the fact that many other contemporary stories, films and other media seem anathema to many of the faithful.

In our contemporary world, then, the quest for the Grail has become the search for good within one's own soul as well as the desire to find some meaning and purpose in the often chaotic and terrifying world around us. In an age when innumerable and overwhelming tales of the darkest reaches of the soul speed around the globe via social media at the merest touch of a fingertip, the quest for the light can seem quixotic at best; and yet, however great our thirst for the news fresh from the dark side, it is counterbalanced in most of us with a yearning for strength to find faith in the forces of light, of good and of justice. The search for the Grail in these dark times – and when are times ever not dark, except in dreams and in visions of a lost golden age? – is the quest for the strength within us to continue to seek a path in the light, no matter how dark the world around us may be. The Holy Grail is, in secular terms, the 'Cup of Hope', and our desire to seek it refreshes our very souls. Hence the stories written and rewritten about the quest for the Grail tap into a recurrent wellspring of deep desire. The figure of Arthur himself, on the other hand, provides a canvas upon which we can paint portraits of our better selves, imperfect perhaps, but still aspirational, and thus his trials, tribulations and failures actually offer us solace at the same time that his unswerving adherence to the ideal good – even in the face of failure and certain destruction – speaks to our own internal and eternal desire to achieve something approaching perfection, both in ourselves and in our world.

# REFERENCES

## Preface: Who was King Arthur?

1 Rodney Castleden, *King Arthur: The Truth Behind the Legend* (London, 2000), pp. 5–7.
2 Christopher A. Snyder, *The World of King Arthur* (New York, 2000), p. 149.
3 Norris J. Lacy, Geoffrey Ashe and Debra N. Mancoff, *The Arthurian Handbook,* 2nd edn (New York, 1997), p. 312.
4 Alan Lupack, *The Oxford Guide to Arthurian Literature and Legend* (Oxford, 2005), p. 13.
5 Lacy et al., *Arthurian Handbook*, pp. 12–13.
6 Richard White, ed., *King Arthur in Legend and History* (New York, 1998), p. 6.
7 Ibid., p. 22.
8 Lupack, *Oxford Guide*, p. 35.
9 Laurie Finke and Martin B. Shichtman, *King Arthur and the Myth of History* (Gainesville, FL, 2004), pp. 38–46.
10 Norma Lorre Goodrich, *King Arthur* (New York, 1986), pp. 41–5.
11 N. J. Higham, *King Arthur: Myth-making and History* (London, 2002), p. 224.
12 White, ed., *Legend and History*, pp. 40–45.
13 Lacy et al., *Arthurian Handbook*, p. 295.
14 Ronan Coghlan, *The Encyclopaedia of Arthurian Legends* (Shaftesbury, Dorset, 1992), p. 82.
15 Lupack, *Oxford Guide*, p. 460.
16 Ibid., p. 29.
17 Lacy et al., *Arthurian Handbook*, p. 122.

## Introduction: Where was Avalon?

1 Norma Lorre Goodrich, *King Arthur* (New York, 1986), pp. 269–73.
2 Flint F. Johnson, *Evidence of Arthur: Fixing the Legendary King in Factual Place and Time* (Jefferson, NC, 2014), pp. 67–70.
3 Alan Lupack, *The Oxford Guide to Arthurian Literature and Legend* (Oxford, 2005), pp. 437–8.
4 Norris J. Lacy, Geoffrey Ashe and Debra N. Mancoff, *The Arthurian Handbook*, 2nd edn (New York, 1997), pp. 294–5.
5 John Barrett, P.W.M. Freeman and Ann Woodward, *Cadbury Castle Somerset: The Later Prehistoric and Early Historic Archaeology* (Swindon, 2000), pp. xiv–xv.
6 Guy Halsall, *Worlds of Arthur: Facts and Fictions of the Dark Ages* (Oxford, 2013), pp. 39–40.
7 Lacy et al., *Arthurian Handbook*, pp. 326–7.
8 Rodney Castleden, *King Arthur: The Truth Behind the Legend* (London, 2000), pp. 167–73.
9 Ibid., pp. 56–69.
10 Steven Morris, 'Tintagel Excavations Reveal Refined Tastes of Medieval Settlers', www.theguardian.com, 13 July 2017.
11 N. J. Higham, *King Arthur: Myth-making and History* (London, 2002), p. 105.
12 Lupack, *Oxford Guide*, p. 433.
13 Christopher A. Snyder, *The World of King Arthur* (New York, 2000), pp. 43–4.
14 Lacy et al., *Arthurian Handbook*, pp. 284–5.
15 Ronan Coghlan, *The Encyclopaedia of Arthurian Legends* (Shaftesbury, Dorset, 1992), p. 42; Lacy et al., *Arthurian Handbook*, p. 285.
16 Richard White, ed., *King Arthur in Legend and History* (New York, 1998), pp. 3–4.
17 Lupack, *Oxford Guide*, p. 14.
18 Halsall, *Worlds of Arthur*, pp. 57–62.
19 Lupack, *Oxford Guide*, pp. 14–15.

## 1 The Lost Gods of Avalon

1 Alan Lupack, *The Oxford Guide to Arthurian Literature and Legend* (Oxford, 2005), p. 476.
2 Norris J. Lacy, Geoffrey Ashe and Debra N. Mancoff, *The Arthurian Handbook*, 2nd edn (New York, 1997), p. 65.
3 James MacKillop, *Dictionary of Celtic Mythology* (Oxford, 1998), pp. 318–19.

4  Ibid., p. 110.
5  Lupack, *Oxford Guide*, pp. 98–9.
6  MacKillop, *Celtic Mythology*, p. 230.
7  Ibid., p. 136.
8  Ronan Coghlan, *The Encyclopaedia of Arthurian Legends* (Shaftesbury, Dorset, 1992), p. 174.
9  Lacy et al., *Arthurian Handbook*, p. 341.
10  MacKillop, *Celtic Mythology*, p. 323.
11  Christopher R. Fee and David Adams Leeming, *Gods, Heroes and Kings: The Battle for Mythic Britain* (Oxford, 2001), p. 188.
12  Coghlan, *Arthurian Legends*, pp. 82–3.
13  MacKillop, *Celtic Mythology*, pp. 4–5.
14  Lupack, *Oxford Guide*, pp. 314–17.
15  Lacy et al., *Arthurian Handbook*, pp. 330–31.
16  Lupack, *Oxford Guide*, pp. 446–7.
17  MacKillop, *Celtic Mythology*, p. 222.
18  Ibid., pp. 152–3.
19  Peter Berresford Ellis, *Dictionary of Celtic Mythology* (Santa Barbara, CA, 1992), p. 111.
20  Lacy et al., *Arthurian Handbook*, p. 291.
21  Ibid., pp. 91–2.
22  Robert W. Hanning and Joan M. Ferrante, *The Lais of Marie De France* (New York, 1978), pp. 23–4.
23  Ibid., pp. 14–15.
24  Lupack, *Oxford Guide*, p. 456.
25  Carl Lindahl, John McNamara and John Lindow, *Medieval Folklore: A Guide to Myths, Legends, Tales, Beliefs and Customs* (Oxford, 2002), pp. 130–31.
26  MacKillop, *Celtic Mythology*, pp. 179–80.
27  Lupack, *Oxford Guide*, pp. 302–4.
28  MacKillop, *Celtic Mythology*, pp. 209–10.
29  Lindahl et al., *Medieval Folklore*, p. 393.
30  Ibid., p. 392.
31  MacKillop, *Celtic Mythology*, p. 210.
32  Lacy et al., *Arthurian Handbook*, pp. 126–8.

## 2 Legendary Treasures of Avalon

1  Alan Lupack, *The Oxford Guide to Arthurian Literature and Legend* (Oxford, 2005), p. 443.
2  James MacKillop, *Dictionary of Celtic Mythology* (Oxford, 1998), pp. 64–5 and 174.

3  Peter Berresford Ellis, *Dictionary of Celtic Mythology* (Santa Barbara, CA, 1992), p. 56.

4  Norris J. Lacy, Geoffrey Ashe and Debra N. Mancoff, *The Arthurian Handbook*, 2nd edn (New York, 1997), p. 306.

5  Ronan Coghlan, *The Encyclopaedia of Arthurian Legends* (Shaftesbury, Dorset, 1992), p. 88.

6  Ellis, *Celtic Mythology*, p. 188.

7  Ibid., p. 192.

8  Lupack, *Oxford Guide*, p. 469.

9  Lacy et al., *Arthurian Handbook*, p. 347.

10  Ibid., p. 345.

11  Lupack, *Oxford Guide*, p. 470.

12  Coghlan, *Arthurian Legends*, p. 199.

13  Lacy et al., *Arthurian Handbook*, pp. 316–18.

14  Lupack, *Oxford Guide*, pp. 448–9.

15  Richard W. Barber, *The Holy Grail: Imagination and Belief* (Cambridge, MA, 2004), pp. 9–26.

16  G. Ronald Murphy, *Gemstone of Paradise: The Holy Grail in Wolfram's Parzival* (Oxford, 2006), pp. 31–6.

17  MacKillop, *Celtic Mythology*, p. 325.

18  Juliette Wood, *Eternal Chalice: The Enduring Legend of the Holy Grail* (London, 2008), pp. 85–105.

19  Barber, *The Holy Grail*, pp. 39–45.

20  Ibid., pp. 153–9.

21  Lupack, *Oxford Guide*, p. 444.

22  Carl Lindahl, John McNamara and John Lindow, *Medieval Folklore: A Guide to Myths, Legends, Tales, Beliefs and Customs* (Oxford, 2002), pp. 184–5.

23  Barber, *The Holy Grail*, pp. 27–38.

24  Coghlan, *Arthurian Legends*, p. 90.

25  Lacy et al., *Arthurian Handbook*, p. 287.

## 3 Arthur Ascendant

1  Alan Lupack, *The Oxford Guide to Arthurian Literature and Legend* (Oxford, 2005), pp. 133–5.

2  Norris J. Lacy, Geoffrey Ashe and Debra N. Mancoff, *The Arthurian Handbook*, 2nd edn (New York, 1997), pp. 351–2.

3  This episode first appears in Robert de Boron's *Merlin*. See Carl Lindahl, John McNamara and John Lindow, *Medieval Folklore: A Guide to Myths, Legends, Tales, Beliefs and Customs* (Oxford, 2002), p. 26.

4 Lindahl et al., *Medieval Folklore*, pp. 377–9.
5 Stephen Knight, *Merlin: Knowledge and Power Through the Ages* (Ithaca, NY, 2009), pp. 1–20.
6 James MacKillop, *Dictionary of Celtic Mythology* (Oxford, 1998), pp. 300–301.
7 Ibid., p. 22.
8 Ibid., p. 258.
9 Ibid., pp. 56–7.
10 Peter Goodrich and Raymond H. Thompson, *Merlin: A Casebook* (New York, 2003), pp. 332–41.
11 Lacy et al., *Arthurian Handbook*, pp. 337–8.
12 MacKillop, *Celtic Mythology*, p. 298.
13 Lupack, *Oxford Guide*, pp. 462–3.
14 Ronan Coghlan, *The Encyclopaedia of Arthurian Legends* (Shaftesbury, Dorset, 1992), pp. 165–6.
15 MacKillop, *Celtic Mythology*, p. 218.
16 Lupack, *Oxford Guide*, p. 440.
17 Ibid., pp. 444–5.
18 Lacy et al., *Arthurian Handbook*, p. 307.
19 Lupack, *Oxford Guide*, pp. 455–6.
20 Coghlan, *Arthurian Legends*, pp. 138–40.
21 Lupack, *Oxford Guide*, p. 460.
22 Ibid., p. 433.
23 Coghlan, *Arthurian Legends*, pp. 164–5.
24 Lacy et al., *Arthurian Handbook*, p. 334.
25 Ibid., p. 337.
26 Lupack, *Oxford Guide*, pp. 461–2.
27 MacKillop, *Celtic Mythology*, p. 65.

## 4 The Once and Present King

1 Alan Lupack, *The Oxford Guide to Arthurian Literature and Legend* (Oxford, 2005), pp. 146–52.
2 Norris J. Lacy, Geoffrey Ashe and Debra N. Mancoff, *The Arthurian Handbook*, 2nd edn (New York, 1997), pp. 158–62.
3 Andrew E. Mathis, *The King Arthur Myth in Modern American Literature* (Jefferson, NC, 2002), pp. 11–12.
4 Lupack, *Oxford Guide*, pp. 162–4.
5 Ibid., p. 164.
6 Ibid., pp. 188–91.
7 Lacy et al., *Arthurian Handbook*, pp. 181–2.
8 Barbara Tepa Lupack, *Adapting the Arthurian Legends for Children: Essays on Arthurian Juvenilia* (New York, 2004), p. 63.

9 John Aberth, *A Knight at the Movies: Medieval History on Film* (New York, 2003), pp. 17–20.
10 Lupack, *Oxford Guide*, pp. 253–4.
11 Tepa Lupack, *Adapting the Arthurian Legends for Children*, p. 288.
12 Aberth, *A Knight at the Movies*, p. 16.
13 Lacy et al., *Arthurian Handbook*, p. 178.
14 Lupack, *Oxford Guide*, pp. 72–4.
15 Sion Barry, 'Bad Wolf to Bring More TV and Film Projects to Wales Following U.S. Investment Boost', www.walesonline.co.uk, 27 March 2017.
16 Susan Lynn Aronstein, *Hollywood Knights: Arthurian Cinema and the Politics of Nostalgia* (New York, 2005), pp. 205–13.
17 Aberth, *A Knight at the Movies*, p. 20.
18 Aronstein, *Hollywood Knights*, pp. 100–106.
19 Martha W. Driver and Sid Ray, *The Medieval Hero on Screen: Representations from Beowulf to Buffy* (Jefferson, NC, 2004), p. 136.
20 Aberth, *A Knight at the Movies*, pp. 16–17.
21 Lupack, *Oxford Guide*, pp. 313–14.
22 Mark Schultz and Thomas Yeates, 'Prince Valiant', www.kingfeatures.com, accessed 20 November 2017.
23 Aronstein, *Hollywood Knights*, pp. 72–7.
24 See www.daysofwonder.com/shadowsovercamelot/en, accessed 21 November 2017.
25 Lupack, *Oxford Guide*, p. 49.
26 Tepa Lupack, *Adapting the Arthurian Legends for Children*, pp. 139–59.
27 Aronstein, *Hollywood Knights*, pp. 122–33.
28 See www.history.com/shows/knightfall/about, accessed 11 November 2017.
29 Aronstein, *Hollywood Knights*, pp. 160–65.
30 For the fullest imaginable Pythonesque treatment of the Grail lore of the Monty Python universe see Darl Larsen, *A Book About the Film 'Monty Python and the Holy Grail': All the References from African Swallows to Zoot* (Lanham, MD, 2015).
31 See http://broadwaymusicalhome.com/shows/spam.htm, accessed 22 November 2017.
32 See www.megcabot.com/avalonhigh, accessed 23 November 2017.
33 See www.abc.go.com/shows/once-upon-a-time/episode-guide, accessed 18 November 2017.
34 Chris Carabott, 'Camelot "Lady of the Lake" Review', www.ign.com, 17 April 2011.

35  Lupack, *Oxford Guide*, pp. 187–8.
36  See www.parenfaire.com/faire/royalarchives.php, accessed
    15 November 2017.
37  Aronstein, *Hollywood Knights*, pp. 133–43.
38  Driver and Ray, *The Medieval Hero on Screen*, p. 176.
39  Veronica Ortenberg, *In Search of the Holy Grail: The Quest for the
    Middle Ages* (London, 2006), pp. 179–82.

## Conclusion: Why does Arthur Abide?

1  See www.kingarthurmovie.com, accessed 19 November 2017.
2  Luke Holland, 'Punish Us, Westeros: Here's How the End of
   Game of Thrones Can Satisfy Fans', www.theguardian.com,
   1 September 2017.

# BIBLIOGRAPHY

Aberth, John, *A Knight at the Movies: Medieval History on Film* (New York, 2003)

Alcock, Leslie, *Arthur's Britain: History and Archaeology* (New York, 2001)

Aronstein, Susan, *Hollywood Knights: Arthurian Cinema and the Politics of Nostalgia* (New York, 2005)

Ashley, Michael, *A Brief History of King Arthur* (London, 2010)

—, *The Mammoth Book of King Arthur* (New York, 2005)

Barber, Richard, *Arthur of Albion* (London, 1961)

—, *The Arthurian Legends* (Totowa, NJ, 1979)

—, *The Holy Grail: Imagination and Belief* (Cambridge, MA, 2004)

Barron, W.R.J., *The Arthur of the English: The Arthurian Legend in Medieval English Life and Literature* (Cardiff, 2001)

Barrowman, R. C., C. E. Batey and C. D. Morris, *Excavations at Tintagel Castle, Cornwall, 1990–1999* (London, 2007)

Batey, Colleen E., *Tintagel Castle* (London, 2016)

BBC News, 'King Arthur's Tintagel "Birthplace" Dig Finds Royal Seat', www.bbc.co.uk, 3 August 2016

Berthelot, Anne, *King Arthur: Chivalry and Legend* (London, 2004)

Bishop, Chris, *Medievalist Comics and the American Century* (Jackson, MS, 2016)

Borroff, Marie, and Laura L. Howes, eds, *Sir Gawain and the Green Knight: An Authoritative Translation, Contexts, Criticism* (New York, 2010)

Bromwich, Rachel, A.O.H. Jarman and Brynley F. Roberts, eds, *The Arthur of the Welsh: The Arthurian Legend in Medieval Welsh Literature* (Cardiff, 1995)

Bulwer, Edward Lytton, *King Arthur: An Epic Poem* (London, 1875)

Burgess, Glyn S., and Karen Pratt, eds, *The Arthur of the French: The Arthurian Legend in Medieval French and Occitan Literature* (Cardiff, 2006)

—, and Keith Busby, trans., *The Lais of Marie De France* (London, 1999)

Burns, John, *King Arthur* (Minehead, 2003)

Butler, Charles, *Four British Fantasists* (New York, 2006)

Cable, James, trans., *The Death of King Arthur* (New York, 1971)

Carr, J. Comyns, *King Arthur: A Drama in a Prologue and Four Acts* (New York, 1895)

Cartlidge, Neil, ed., *Heroes and Anti-heroes in Medieval Romance* (Cambridge, 2012)

Castleden, Rodney, *King Arthur: The Truth Behind the Legend* (New York, 2003)

Chrétien de Troyes, *Arthurian Romances*, trans. William W. Kibler and Carleton W. Carroll (London, 1991)

Clary, Michael, *Excalibur* (Brentwood, TN, 2014)

Coghlan, Ronan, *The Encyclopedia of Arthurian Legends* (Shaftesbury, Dorset, 1991)

Cooper, Helen, ed., *Le Morte D'Arthur* (Oxford, 1998)

Copestake, Timothy, and Francis Pryor, *King Arthur's Britain* (Bethesda MD, 2005)

Corley, Corin, trans., *Lancelot of the Lake* (Oxford, 2000)

Craik, Dinah Maria Mulock, *King Arthur: Not a Love Story* (New York, 1886)

Crossley-Holland, Kevin, and Peter Malone, *The World of King Arthur and his Court: People, Places, Legend and Lore* [1998] (New York, 2004)

Dale, Liam, and Sue Hosler, *Arthur: The Truth Behind the Legend* (Los Angeles, CA, 2004)

Daley, Jason, 'A Palace Was Unearthed Where Legend Places King Arthur's Birthplace', www.smithsonianmag.com, 5 August 2016

Driver, Martha W., and Sid Ray, eds, *The Medieval Hero on Screen: Representations from Beowulf to Buffy* (London, 2004)

Dunning, Robert W., *King Arthur* (Wellington, 2010)

Dykema, Dale K., *King Arthur: The Story of King Arthur and His Knights by Howard Pyle: A Reader's Guide* (Sussex, 2000)

Fermer, David, and Matthias Pflügner, *King Arthur* (Stuttgart, 2012)

Finke, Laurie A., and Martin B. Shichtman, *King Arthur and the Myth of History* (Gainesville, FL, 2009)

Gantz, Jeffrey, trans., *The Mabinogion* (New York, 1976)

Goodman, Jennifer, *The Legend of Arthur in British and American Literature* (Boston, MA, 1988)

Goodrich, Norma Lorre, *King Arthur* (London, 1989)

Goodrich, Peter H., and Raymond H. Thompson, *Merlin: A Casebook* (London, 2003)

Greaney, Susan, 'Discoveries and Excavations at Tintagel Castle: Summer 2016', http://blog.english-heritage.org.uk, 5 August 2016

Halsall, Guy, *Worlds of Arthur: Facts and Fictions of the Dark Ages* (Oxford, 2013)

Harty, Kevin J., *The Reel Middle Ages: American, Western and Eastern European, Middle Eastern, and Asian Films about Medieval Europe* (Jefferson, NC, and London, 1999)

Hennig, Kaye D., and Jan Howarth, *King Arthur: Lord of the Grail* (Friday Harbor, WA, 2008)

Higham, N. J., *King Arthur: Myth-making and History* (New York, 2002)

—, *King Arthur: Pocket Giants* (Stroud, 2015)

Hunt, August, *King Arthur: Shadows in the Mist* (London, 2010)

Jackson. W. H., and S. A. Ranawake, eds, *The Arthur of the Germans: The Arthurian Legend in Medieval German and Dutch Literature* (Cardiff, 2000)

Johnson, Flint F., *Evidence of Arthur: Fixing the Legendary King in Factual Place and Time* (London, 2014)

Kalinke, Marianne E., ed., *The Arthur of the North: The Arthurian Legend in the Norse and Rus' Realms* (Cardiff, 2011)

Kennedy, Edward Donald, *King Arthur: A Casebook* (New York and London, 1996)

Kibler, William W., trans., *Arthurian Romances* (New York, 1991)

Kieckhefer, Richard, *Magic in the Middle Ages* (Cambridge, 1989)

Knight, Owen, *King Arthur: An Astral King* (New Orleans, LA, 2012)

Knight, Stephen, *Arthurian Literature and Society* (New York, 1983)

—, *Merlin: Knowledge and Power Through the Ages* (Ithaca, NY, 2009)

Lacy, Norris J., and Geoffrey Ashe, *The Arthurian Handbook* (New York, 1997)

—, and James J. Wilhelm, eds, *The Romance of Arthur: An Anthology of Medieval Texts in Translation* (New York, 2013)

Lagorio, Valerie Marie, and Mildred Leake Day, *King Arthur through the Ages* (New York, 1990)

Larsen, Darl, *A Book about the Film 'Monty Python and the Holy Grail': All the References from African Swallows to Zoot* (London, 2015)

Laubenthal, Anne Sanders, *Excalibur* (New York, 1973)

Lawrence-Mathers, Anne, *The True History of Merlin the Magician* (New Haven, CT, 2012)

Lupack, Alan, *The Oxford Guide to Arthurian Literature and Legend* (Oxford, 2005)

Lupack, Barbara Tepa, ed., *Adapting the Arthurian Legends for Children: Essays on Arthurian Juvenilia* (New York, 2004)

Lyle, Anthony, *King Arthur: Pendragon* (Victoria, British Columbia, 2012)

Malory, Thomas, and Stephen H. A. Shepherd, *Le Morte Darthur or The Hoole Book of Kyng Arthur and of His Noble Knyghtes of the Rounde Table: Authoritative Text, Sources and Backgrounds, Criticism* (New York, 2004)

Matarasso, Pauline Maud, ed., *The Quest of the Holy Grail* (London, 1969)

Mathis, Andrew E., *The King Arthur Myth in Modern American Literature* (London, 2002)

Mersey, Daniel, and Alan Lathwell, *King Arthur: Myths and Legends* (Oxford, 2013)

—, and Alan Lathwell, *The Knights of the Round Table: Myths and Legends* (Oxford, 2015)

Moll, Richard J., *Before Malory: Reading Arthur in Later Medieval England* (Toronto, 2003)

Murphy, G. Ronald, *Gemstone of Paradise: The Holy Grail in Wolfram's 'Parzival'* (Oxford, 2006)

Nastali, Dan, 'Swords, Grails, and Bag-puddings: A Survey of Children's Poetry and Plays', in *Adapting the Arthurian Legends for Children*, ed. Barbara Lupack (New York, 2004), pp. 171–96

Nolen, Shannon, *Mythological Heroes and Saviors: King Arthur* (Austin, TX, 2012)

Ortenberg, Veronica, *In Search of the Holy Grail: The Quest for the Middle Ages* (London, 2006)

Ouwehand, Maaike, *King Arthur: A Legend's Influence on Aspects of Tourism* (Breda, 2004)

Phillips, Arthur, *The Tragedy of Arthur* (New York, 2011)

Phillips, Graham, and Martin Keatman, *King Arthur: The True Story* (London, 2012)

Purcell, Henry, and John Dryden, *King Arthur* (London, 1691)

Pyle, Howard, *The Story of King Arthur and His Knights* (New York, 1909)

Reid, Margaret, *The Arthurian Legend* (New York, 1961)

Romey, Kristin, 'Not-so-dark Ages Revealed at King Arthur Site', www.nationalgeographic.com, 10 August 2016

Snyder, Christopher A., *Exploring the World of King Arthur* (London, 2000)

—, *The Britons* (Malden, MA, 2003)

Spivack, Charlotte, 'Susan Cooper's "The Dark is Rising"', in *Adapting the Arthurian Legends for Children*, ed. Barbara T. Lupack (New York, 2004), pp. 161–9

Stang, Gesa, *King Arthur: Cyan-Projekt* (Leipzig, 2003)

Taylor, Beverly, and Elisabeth Brewer, *The Return of King Arthur* (Cambridge, 1983)

Thomas, Gwyn, and Margaret Jones, *King Arthur* (Talybont, 2006)

—, and Jenny Nimmo, *King Arthur* (Cardiff, 2000)

Thompson, Frank T., *King Arthur* (New York, 2004)

Thompson, Raymond H., 'Interview with Susan Cooper', in *Adapting the Arthurian Legends for Children*, ed. Barbara T. Lupack (New York, 2004), pp. 139–59

—, 'The Sense of Place in Arthurian Fiction for Younger Readers', in *Adapting the Arthurian Legends for Children*, ed. Barbara T. Lupack (New York, 2004), pp. 123–38

—, 'The Enchanter Awakes: Merlin in Modern Fiction', in *Merlin: A Casebook*, ed. Peter H. Goodrich and Raymond H. Thompson (New York, 2003), pp. 250–62

Thorpe, Lewis, trans., *The History of the Kings of Britain* (New York, 1966)

Twain, Mark, *A Connecticut Yankee in King Arthur's Court* (New York, 1889)

White, Paul, *King Arthur: Man or Myth?* (Launceston, 2000)

White, Richard, ed., *King Arthur in Legend and History* (New York, 1998)

Whyte, Jack, *Excalibur* (London, 2013)

Wood, Juliette, *Eternal Chalice: The Enduring Legend of the Holy Grail* (London, 2008)

# FURTHER READING
# AND FILMOGRAPHY

## Editions of Primary Sources

Borroff, Marie, and Laura L. Howes, eds, *Sir Gawain and the Green Knight: An Authoritative Translation, Contexts, Criticism* (New York, 2010)

Chrétien de Troyes, *Arthurian Romances*, trans. William W. Kibler and Carleton W. Carroll (London, 1991)

Gantz, Jeffrey, trans., *The Mabinogion* (New York, 1976)

Geoffrey of Monmouth and Lewis Thorpe, *The History of the Kings of Britain* (New York, 1966)

Lacy, Norris J., and James J. Wilhelm, eds, *The Romance of Arthur: An Anthology of Medieval Texts in Translation* (New York, 2013)

Malory, Thomas, and Stephen H. A. Shepherd, *Le Morte Darthur or The Hoole Book of Kyng Arthur and of His Noble Knyghtes of the Rounde Table: Authoritative Text, Sources and Backgrounds, Criticism* (New York, 2004)

Marie de France, *The Lais of Marie de France*, intro. Keith Busby, trans. Glyn Burgess (London, 1999)

## General Arthurian Reference Works

Alcock, Leslie, *Arthur's Britain: History and Archaeology* (New York, 2001)

Barber, Richard, *The Arthurian Legends* (Totowa, NJ, 1979)

Coghlan, Ronan, *The Encyclopedia of Arthurian Legends* (Shaftesbury, Dorset, 1991)

Finke, Laurie A., and Martin B. Shichtman, *King Arthur and the Myth of History* (Gainesville, FL, 2009)

Goodrich, Norma Lorre, *King Arthur* (London, 1989)

Higham, N. J., *King Arthur: Myth-making and History* (New York, 2002)

Lacy, Norris J., and Geoffrey Ashe, *The Arthurian Handbook* (New York, 1997)

Lupack, Alan, *The Oxford Guide to Arthurian Literature and Legend* (Oxford, 2005)

Snyder, Christopher A., *Exploring the World of King Arthur* (London, 2000)

White, Richard, ed., *King Arthur in Legend and History* (New York, 1998)

## The Historical Arthur

Batey, Colleen E., *Tintagel Castle* (London, 2016)

BBC News, 'King Arthur's Tintagel "Birthplace" Dig Finds Royal Seat', www.bbc.com, 3 August 2016

Castleden, Rodney, *King Arthur: The Truth Behind the Legend* (New York, 2003)

Daley, Jason, 'A Palace Was Unearthed Where Legend Places King Arthur's Birthplace', www.smithsonianmag.com, 5 August 2016

Greaney, Susan, 'Discoveries and Excavations at Tintagel Castle: Summer 2016', http://blog.english-heritage.org.uk, 5 August 2016

Halsall, Guy, *Worlds of Arthur: Facts and Fictions of the Dark Ages* (Oxford, 2013)

Johnson, Flint F., *Evidence of Arthur: Fixing the Legendary King in Factual Place and Time* (London, 2014)

Romey, Kristin, 'Not-so-dark Ages Revealed at King Arthur Site', http://news.nationalgeographic.com, 10 August 2016

## Arthur in Popular Culture

Aberth, John, *A Knight at the Movies: Medieval History on Film* (New York, 2003)

Aronstein, Susan, *Hollywood Knights: Arthurian Cinema and the Politics of Nostalgia* (New York, 2005)

Bishop, Chris, *Medievalist Comics and the American Century* (Jackson, MS, 2016)

Driver, Martha W., and Sid Ray, eds, *The Medieval Hero on Screen: Representations from Beowulf to Buffy* (London, 2004)

Goodman, Jennifer, *The Legend of Arthur in British and American Literature* (Boston, MA, 1988)

Larsen, Darl, *A Book About the Film 'Monty Python and the Holy Grail': All the References from African Swallows to Zoot* (London, 2015)

Lupack, Barbara Tepa, ed., *Adapting the Arthurian Legends for Children: Essays on Arthurian Juvenilia* (New York, 2004)

Mathis, Andrew E., *The King Arthur Myth in Modern American*
  *Literature* (London, 2002)


## The Holy Grail

Barber, Richard, *The Holy Grail: Imagination and Belief*
  (Cambridge, MA, 2004)
Murphy, G. Ronald, *Gemstone of Paradise: The Holy Grail in Wolfram's*
  *'Parzival'* (Oxford, 2006)
Ortenberg, Veronica, *In Search of the Holy Grail: The Quest for the*
  *Middle Ages* (London, 2006)
Wood, Juliette, *Eternal Chalice: The Enduring Legend of the Holy*
  *Grail* (London, 2008)


## Merlin

Goodrich, Peter H., and Raymond H. Thompson, *Merlin:*
  *A Casebook* (London, 2003)
Knight, Stephen, *Merlin: Knowledge and Power Through the Ages*
  (Ithaca, NY, 2009)


## Selected Arthurian Adaptations

Cochran, Molly, and Warren Murphy, *The Forever King*
  (New York, 1992)
—, and Warren Murphy, *The Broken Sword* (New York, 1997)
—, and Warren Murphy, *The Third Magic* (New York, 2003)
Cooper, Susan, *Over Sea, Under Stone* (New York, 1965)
—, *The Dark is Rising* (New York, 1973)
—, *The Grey King* (New York, 1975)
—, *Silver on the Tree* (New York, 1977)
—, *Greenwitch* (New York, 1997)
Cornwell, Bernard, *The Winter King: A Novel of Arthur* (London, 1995)
—, *Enemy of God: A Novel of Arthur* (London, 1996)
—, *Excalibur: A Novel of Arthur* (London, 1997)
Stewart, Mary, *The Crystal Cave* (New York, 1970)
—, *The Hollow Hills* (New York, 1973)
—, *The Last Enchantment* (New York, 1979)
—, *The Wicked Day* (New York, 1983)
Tennyson, Alfred, *Idylls of the King*, ed. J. M. Gray [1859]
  (New York, 1989)
Twain, Mark, *A Connecticut Yankee in King Arthur's Court:*
  *An Authoritative Text, Backgrounds and Sources, Composition*

*and Publication Criticism*, ed. Allison R. Ensor [1889]
(New York, 1982)
White, T. H., *The Once and Future King* [1958] (New York, 1987)
—, *The Book of Merlyn* [1977] (Austin, TX, 1987)

# A Selected Arthurian Filmography

*A Connecticut Yankee in King Arthur's Court*, dir. Tay Garnett
(Paramount Pictures, 1949)
*Lancelot and Guinevere*, dir. Cornel Wilde (Universal International
Films, 1963)
*The Sword in the Stone*, dir. Wolfgang Reitherman
(Walt Disney Pictures, 1963)
*Camelot*, dir. Joshua Logan (Warner Bros-Seven Arts, 1967)
*Monty Python and the Holy Grail*, dir. Terry Gilliam and Terry Jones
(EMI Films, 1975)
*Excalibur*, dir. John Boorman (Warner Bros, 1981)
*Knightriders*, dir. George A. Romero (United Artists, 1981)
*Indiana Jones and the Last Crusade*, dir. Steven Spielberg
(Paramount Pictures, 1989)
*The Fisher King*, dir. Terry Gilliam (Tri-Star Pictures, 1991)
*A Kid in King Arthur's Court*, dir. Michael Gottlieb (Walt Disney
Pictures, 1995)
*Ancient Mysteries: Camelot, Extraordinary Breakthroughs in the Search
for the Legendary Camelot*, dir. Michael Cascio (A&E TV, 1995)
*First Knight*, dir. Jerry Zucker (Columbia Pictures, 1995)
*Merlin*, dir. Steve Barron (Hallmark Entertainment, 1998)
*Quest for Camelot*, dir. Frederik Du Chau (Warner Bros, 1998)
*The Mists of Avalon*, dir. Uli Edel (TNT, 2001)
*King Arthur*, dir. Antoine Fuqua (Buena Vista Pictures, 2004)
*Biography: King Arthur: His Life and Legends*, dir. Sue Hayes
(A&E, 2005)
*King Arthur's Britain*, dir. Francis Pryor (Acorn Media, 2005)
*Merlin's Apprentice*, dir. David Wu (Hallmark Entertainment, 2006)
*Merlin*, dir. James Hawes (BBC One, 2008)
*Avalon High*, dir. Stuart Gillard (Disney-ABC Television, 2010)
*The Sorcerer's Apprentice*, dir. Jon Turteltaub (Walt Disney Pictures,
2010)
*Camelot*, created by Chris Chibnall and Michael Hurst (Starz, 2011)
*King Arthur and Medieval Britain*, dir. History Channel
(A&E Entertainment, 2012)
*King Arthur: Legend of the Sword*, dir. Guy Ritchie (Warner Bros, 2017)

# ACKNOWLEDGEMENTS

I must thank my many students, especially those in my medieval mythology, British mythology and medieval epic courses, on whom I have tested material from this book and who have made it amply clear what worked and what didn't. I most especially owe thanks to the students in my spring 2017 course on King Arthur, who read draft chapters of this book, and whose own papers, presentations and perspectives informed my views on contemporary manifestations of Arthurian myths and legends. These young collaborators include E. Anderson, S. Braat, R. Campo, K. Hoehn, S. Hossain, D. Jahn, A. Kamppila, K. Kochanowicz, A. Link, S. Misurell, N. Petrocchi, S. Rinehart, K. Rubinstein, E. Smith and H. Theurer. Moreover, I owe special debts of gratitude to my able student research assistants Maggie Stein and Jerome Clarke: Maggie was especially helpful in the initial stages of the project and most particularly in the compilation of the Bibliography, while Jerome stepped in to help develop and manage aspects of my Arthurian course, and also travelled to Britain with me to capture images of Arthurian sites. I would be remiss if I did not also mention Casey Chwieko, children's librarian extraordinaire, whose senior honors thesis on Arthurian themes in young adult literature set me on a path to visit a number of works discussed in my final chapter. Great thanks are also due to the English Department at Gettysburg College, and especially to our office administrator Jody Rosensteel, along with my colleagues Betsy Duquette, Suzanne Flynn, Kent Gramm and most especially Ian Clarke, a true friend who critiqued a draft of the manuscript in its entirety. I would also like to thank my friend and colleague Jim Udden, in Film Studies; the Provost's Office; and the college's Faculty Development Committee. I should also mention Ben, Michael and Rebecca at Reaktion Books, who have been extremely supportive since the inception of this project. I must acknowledge that I first began exploring the realms of Arthur for my final paper for John Duffy, my senior honors English teacher at St Edward High School; Mr

Duffy is the yardstick by which I measure my success as a teacher to this very day. Along similar lines, I owe a shout-out to Jeanne Haile, who typed the first draft of this book 35 years ago as of this writing, almost to the day. Last, but hardly least, I must thank my wife Allison Singley, my boon companion on many an adventure in Avalon and beyond.

## Photo Acknowledgements

The author and the publishers wish to express their thanks to the below sources of illustrative material and/or permission to reproduce it.

All images © Jerome Clarke & Christopher R. Fee 2017 except the following: © The British Library, London: pp. 6, 10, 15, 50, 57, 69, 72, 84, 87, 93, 96, 102, 107, 112, 114, 130, 139, 142, 143, 147, 169, 179, 186; Christopher Finot: p. 89; iStockphoto: p. 22 (duncan1890); Library of Congress, Washington, DC: p. 155.

# INDEX

Page numbers in *italics* refer to illustrations